PRAISE FOR

Peace

"*Peace* equips you to fight anxiety and worry with God's truth. Through guided prayers, manifestos, and Scripture, *Peace* gives readers tools that can change their lives and the lives of their families."

—ALLI WORTHINGTON, author *of Standing Strong: A Woman's Guide to Overcoming Adversity and Living with Confidence*, speaker, and business coach

"As I navigate the unexpected pain of pregnancy loss, *Peace* is the resource my anxious mama heart has needed. Becky has provided a powerful, much-needed tool to equip mothers with confidence and unshakable faith in all stages of parenting, and I am thankful."

—JORDAN LEE DOOLEY, national bestselling author *of Own Your Everyday: Overcome the Pressure to Prove and Show Up for What You Were Made to Do*

Peace

Peace

. . . .

HOPE AND HEALING FOR THE ANXIOUS MOMMA'S HEART

Becky Thompson

WATERBROOK

PEACE

This book is not intended to replace the advice of a trained psychological or medical professional. Readers are advised to consult a qualified professional regarding treatment. The author and publisher specifically disclaim liability, loss, or risk, personal or otherwise, which is incurred as a consequence, directly or indirectly, of the use or application of any of the contents of this book.

LIBRARY OF CONGRESS CATALOGING-IN-PUBLICATION DATA
Names: Thompson, Becky (Rebecca F.), author.
Title: Peace : hope and healing for the anxious momma's heart / Becky Thompson.
Description: First edition. | [Colorado Springs, CO] : WaterBrook, 2020.
Identifiers: LCCN 2019054874 | ISBN 9780525652694 (trade paperback) | ISBN 9780525652700 (ebook)
Subjects: LCSH: Motherhood—Religious aspects—Christianity.
Mothers—Religious life. | Peace—Religious aspects—Christianity. |
Anxiety—Religious aspects—Christianity.
Classification: LCC BV4529.18 .T4666 2020 | DDC 248.8/431—dc23
LC record available at https://lccn.loc.gov/2019054874

Printed in the United States of America on acid-free paper

waterbrookmultnomah.com

2 4 6 8 9 7 5 3 1

First Edition

SPECIAL SALES

For Kadence

Foreword

....

"Dad, I had no idea . . ."

My daughter's voice trailed off. As her parent, I knew what Megan was going to say before she even finished. We were standing in the nursery belonging to my brand-new granddaughter, Olivia (who I call Papa Girl), surrounded by the baby decor that had been lovingly selected months before by Megan and Ben and my wife, Julie. The arrangement of stuffed elephants, the baby books, and the warm blankets on the rocking chair—gifts from family members and friends in honor of "Princess O"—signified the hours Megan spent preparing to welcome her first child.

I felt my heart beat in my chest as Megan continued, "Dad, I know you always said how much you loved and cared for us, and I always knew how much you loved me. But I didn't fully understand until now."

I smiled at my daughter—now a mom—who has always made us so proud. And I thought about how love does nothing but grow even more over the years.

The love of a parent is fierce. And this love is so forgiving and wildly sacrificing. It will make your heart soar and sink in the same day—or sometimes in the same hour. This powerful love also makes us vulnerable because we can't control everything for our children in this broken world, and there's nothing more terrifying than that for a loving parent. We can't control the possibility of our kids getting high fevers, dying from SIDS, choking, falling and getting hurt, being late, being made fun of and bullied, getting lost or taken, not making the team, getting disappointing grades . . . and on and on. Each stage brings its own challenges, stressors, and insanity of sorts.

For Christian parents, it's a lifetime of calling on God's protection, comfort, and wisdom to help us navigate our feelings and responsibility. For some, that vulnerability can become a deep, painful battle rooted in all-consuming anxiety. I have sat with parents who love and trust the Lord with all their hearts but also battle crippling fear related to parenthood. This fear can keep them up at night or make them tired all day. It can affect their personalities so much—with tears and anger triggers around every corner—that even their spouses don't recognize them anymore. And, oh, how it can steal joy.

But no matter how tightly fear has gripped your heart, it doesn't have to stay that way. You can loosen the grip. Maybe not on your own, but with loving counsel and persistent prayer and by inviting Christ into your darkest places, you can win this battle and overcome. You can be free to love deeply and parent well.

I want you to know that if you picked up this book as a lifeline or an anchor in your journey as a parent, there is hope and healing. It comes moored in a relationship with our heavenly Father, who sent His own Son—His dearly loved Son—into our brokenness and pain. Taking the first step to reach out starts the healing journey.

Through the years, I've watched multitudes of parents work through their consuming fears to find a way to live unburdened and free from the weight that once gripped them. What Becky has written in this work is biblically sound, deeply encouraging, and filled with wisdom that will speak to your heart. You can be the mom God wants you to be and the loving, emotionally close mom your kids need. Know that God's heart is toward you as you begin.

DR. TIM CLINTON
President of the American Association of
Christian Counselors

Contents

. . . .

To You, Momma, Before We Begin

....

Hi there! I know you. Well, I don't know your name, but I know you better than you might think. You picked up this book or downloaded it onto your device or you're listening to the audio version because we are alike. It's just that simple. If you didn't face anxiety at some point in your life or hadn't ever felt overwhelmed by everything or nothing at all, then I don't believe you would have found your way to this book. So, right here at the beginning, I want you to know that I get it. I know how it feels to live with an underscore of anxiety as the soundtrack of your life.

I also know what it's like to be told to just stop feeling the way I do. I've had people say to me, "Just stop worrying. Just pray more or read more Scripture or focus on what's good and you'll *get better.*" As if, perhaps, I hadn't thought of doing those things. Or, worse, as if maybe I just wasn't doing those things well enough.

I understand what it's like to love the Lord and read the Bible and know that God is good and trustworthy and completely deserving of our full faith. To *know* that His Word says "Be anxious for nothing"[1] yet *feel* anxious about everything. I know what it's like to be a Christian woman battling the sickness of anxiety. And I know that more than anything, if you're like me at all, you crave peace above everything else and reassurance that there's not something broken with your faith because you can't shake the fear.

So, before I tell you my story and we go on this journey together, I want to be sure you know a few things from the start. First, you, with all the forms of anxiousness you experience, are welcome here. I don't know your story. I don't know what you've been through, when the fear started, what caused it, or what triggers it today. I don't know how you manage it or whether you've told anyone about it. I don't know whether you're just hoping the fear passes on its own or you've tried everything to no avail. But I do know that you don't need to be anything other than who you really are to find hope and healing in these words. I just need you to be honest with how you've felt, what you've thought, and what you've believed. And I need you to be okay with me being very honest in what I share with you.

I believe in honesty. I believe in the power of sharing our stories. And I believe that you are living a story right now that others are going to need to hear about someday. It's true. I believe every road we walk has pieces of our story that Jesus invites us to gather as we journey. Think of every road Jesus walked. Each step He took taught us, inspired us, and pointed us toward our Father in heaven. Even the road that led to the cross told the ultimate story of God's sacrificial love.

The road you find yourself on today isn't a path you alone will walk. Women will come behind you, maybe this year or years from now, who will need to know how you made it.

They are going to need to hear how you became healthy and found both acceptance of the story you're living and freedom from the power of fear in your life. Maybe these women will not hear you share your story from a stage or read it in the form of a book (but maybe they will!). Maybe you'll share your story across cups of coffee or over the phone late at night or through a text to another desperate momma. But no matter how you end up using your journey and your story, this road you are walking right now just might save someone else's life. That's powerful. *That's heavy.*

I've said it before in other books, but I think it needs to be repeated here: seasons often seem hard and weighty because we don't realize how many women we are carrying with us— women who will learn or grow or be healed because we walked the road in front of us, carrying their hope within our own stories, taking notes along the path, and leaving a trail of courage for them to follow.

We have the chance to influence so many people when we acknowledge the stories God is writing in our lives, even the hardest parts, and then find the bravery to share them with others. So, I hope you underline or highlight or take some notes as we journey together through this book. I hope you start to prepare to share what God has done and is doing in you as we walk toward peace.

Next, I need you to know that we are on the same team. Always. Forever. You and me. I have never written a book for a woman I didn't believe could be my best friend. All the advice or hope or truth that I share through all platforms is intended for women I could go out and get a coffee with (if we could find someone to watch our children). I think of us together as I write these words to you. The Lord asked me to share these words with you, so I imagine you every time I sit down to write them.

As a matter of fact, I had this vision of you while I was standing at my kitchen sink one night about a year ago. I say vision, but I didn't see anything with my eyes. I wasn't praying or meditating on God's Word. I wasn't alone or in deep, reflective thought. Actually, I was finally soaping the dishes I had been avoiding all day when I looked out into my backyard and saw a whole scene playing out in my mind as if I were watching a movie I had seen a million times.

As I scrubbed a pan, I saw this woman. I couldn't describe her face or tell you her age or ethnicity. I just knew she was a woman who was afraid. She was standing in the middle of a dark forest, blindfolded as if she had been kidnapped and dropped off in the woods by her captor. She couldn't see anything; she could just hear the sounds around her. Rustling leaves. Wind in the trees. Her own quick breathing. Her heart pounded inside her chest, and I watched as she reached up and slowly pulled the covering from her eyes, trembling and terrified of what she'd see.

Her breathing quickened. I could tell she was panicked. She blinked, and as the fuzziness cleared, she peered into the darkness, beginning to make sense of her surroundings. It was night. The only light came from the moon shining through the tops of the trees. She spun one way and then the other. But there was only forest in all directions. Only night. Only cold darkness.

"Helloooo?" she cried out as panic took over. She paused and listened. "Hello!?" she called out again, allowing her plea to ring out in the night air as if she were a little girl awakened from a bad dream. But this was no dream. This was the dark forest of fear and anxiety in the middle of the night, and she had no idea how she was going to get out of there alive.

Tears streamed down my face as I rinsed out a glass. "Lord, who is she?" I asked, heartbroken for this woman who felt so desperately alone.

And the Lord answered, *She's a woman lost in the forest of fear, and you're going back for her so we can lead her out together.*

"Okay," I answered through hot tears. "Tell her I'm coming, Lord! Help her see she's not alone!" At the time, I was in an intense season of anxiety. I was living daily with that familiar weight of worry that steals all the extra space in my heart. I've lived with anxiety most of my life, but some seasons have been harder than others. And as the Lord showed me this vision, I knew this time my walk through the woods would be different. This time I was to take notes of how I navigated certain situations. I was to make a map that I could use to lead other women out of the forest of fear.

Listen to me, sister. I'm not a psychologist. I'm not a licensed counselor or a therapist. I have no training that would qualify me to give you any medical or professional advice. I will not claim that I am someone the medical world would recommend as a resource on this subject. But I have spent years navigating a life with anxiety. I am on the inside of this story. And so, whether you have lived in the darkness of anxiety most of your life or it seems as though you've been kidnapped by your emotions and dropped off suddenly without cause or explanation, I know these woods. I know how fear likes to lead, how it taunts, how it tries to make your mind play tricks on you. I know how hopeless the space you're in right now can feel. And if there was ever a guide who knows this path well enough to tell you how to find peace in the middle of fear, it's me, following the Holy Spirit as our ultimate guide.

Friend, there are so many reasons you might be experiencing anxiety right now. You might be able to pinpoint a cause or a catalyst that brought you to this place. Or maybe you can't. Maybe you have always been just a little bit afraid. Maybe you have always been just a little bit anxious. Or maybe you're looking around, asking yourself, *How did I get here?*

Sister, more important than knowing how you got here is knowing the way out. It's knowing where to place your feet and what to trust as solid ground as you journey through this space. That's what we're going to work through together.

I need to be clear about something. We aren't formulating a personalized plan for you to overcome the anxiety you face, because our methods to finding wholeness are all unique. In the pages ahead, we are going to identify solid places for your heart to find rest and meet with Jesus as you journey forward. So much of our fear is rooted in lies we've believed about ourselves or about who God is. And while I don't have the clinical recommendations to tell you how to stop your racing heart, I do have the biblical foundation—and a degree to back it—to give your feet a safe place to walk. So, we are going to look at spiritual, mental, emotional, physical, and practical steps we can take together that will lead us to hope and healing.

You're much less alone than you feel. You're much closer to Jesus than it seems. And so many of us out here understand exactly what it feels like not only to deal with constant anxiety but also to navigate motherhood at the same time. There is hope for us. There is healing for us. And, friend, I venture to say there is even peace for our troubled hearts. It's our aim. It's our focus. It's the center of this book and the foundation under each step I'm going to invite you to take with me.

Peace is not just an idea. It's not just a goal. Peace is a person. We're on a journey to walk with Peace Himself right through that forest of fear until the dawn breaks and we reach the clearing.

Peace

Unafraid of the Dark

WHAT DOES THE FEAR YOU FEEL SAY ABOUT YOUR FAITH?

About a year ago, I woke up one morning and felt nervous about everything but nothing specific. I closed my eyes and tried to remember what I was worried about exactly. We had made a cross-country move from Oklahoma to California on a giant God adventure just about six months before. Despite the big leap, our kids were settling into school and life in Los Angeles. Our marriage was in a really healthy place. Our business was steadily growing. Our finances weren't in terrible shape. We had supportive families and a growing community, and we had never felt more strongly that God was leading us daily. He was meeting all our needs, but despite how great everything seemed, that morning I woke up afraid.

Here's the way I describe this sort of feeling to friends or family who don't deal with chronic anxiety: Imagine your alarm clock goes off and you open your eyes, knowing you're going to face something that day that will bring you to a fearful place. It's the same feeling someone might experience if she was afraid of the dentist and had a nine o'clock appointment, if she was about to take a big exam she didn't feel prepared for, or if she needed to make a speech and was terrified of public speaking.

Anxiety can feel just like those common fears anyone might experience when anticipating a big event or when an uncomfortable situation needs to be overcome. It's the feeling of getting ready to face something scary, but there's not always a specific cause on the calendar. Sometimes it's brought on by something specific we are afraid of, but other times it's not. There's no dentist appointment or exam or speech. There's not always even a conversation or conflict. Nothing needs to be tackled, climbed, surmounted, or pushed through. There's just fear. Looming fear. About everything. And nothing. And sometimes that feeling of fear can be scary all on its own.

Why? Well, those of us with anxiety know that when the average person has fear about the dentist appointment, she can look forward to the appointment being over. When she must give the speech or take the test or sit through the interview, once it's done, it's done. But when fear comes without a cause, we don't have that hope of getting to the other side of the situation. There's no deep sigh of relief and release of stress once it's done and over with. There's just the lingering unrest of an unidentified dread. And in that restless place of worry, we can begin to look for and create unrealistic fears that feel very, very real.

That's how I felt that morning one year ago. My heart sank. It was as though something terrible had happened or was about to happen, yet everything was just about as good as it could be. My brain was signaling to my body some impending doom, something off, something that deserved my attention. But I couldn't think of what it could be.

Like flipping through files, I pulled up in my mind each person I love, doing my best to locate the source of the morning's fear. *Is everything okay with Jared?* I couldn't think of anything wrong with my husband. *It's not him. What about Kolton or Kadence or Jaxton?* I thought of each of my children's faces. Nothing to be afraid of. Well, nothing out of the ordinary sprang to the front of my thoughts . . . just all the usual worries a typical mom might have concerning her children.

I continued to think of situations and relationships, work deadlines and friendships, and I couldn't identify any one thing that could be causing this sinking feeling of fear. Simply, I had nothing to be worried about, yet I was nervous about the day.

I wonder if you've ever experienced something similar. Yes, I'm sure we can all say we have gone to bed thinking about a problem that causes us to feel afraid and then awoken the next morning with the same issue ready to reclaim our attention. Maybe for you it was a health situation or financial issue. Maybe it was a relationship in conflict or a conversation that needed to be had. Maybe it was work or something to do with your husband or with your child's teacher. Maybe it was just your daily to-do list that seemed so much bigger than you. But maybe, like me, you've woken up and experienced fear without a source. You've felt alarmed by . . . something . . . everything . . . but nothing at all. Maybe you've just felt anxious.

What Is Anxiety?

....

Many of us are familiar with the feeling, but few of us understand what actually goes on in our bodies when we experience anxiety. So, what is anxiety, exactly? According to the
American Psychiatric Association, "Anxiety is a normal reaction to stress.... It can alert us to dangers and help us prepare and pay attention.... Anxiety refers to anticipation of a
future concern."[1] Basically, anxiety is what we experience
when we look toward the future and feel afraid and then prepare to face whatever threat we see coming. Anxiety disorders are different from daily feelings of nervousness. Anxiety
disorders are diagnosed when a person's fear is not propor-
tional to the situation he's facing and when his responses to
the fear impede his daily life.[2]

I know how anxious momma hearts work. If I had just
read those facts surrounding anxiety disorders, I would start
self-diagnosing, wondering, *Do I have a disorder? Am I okay?*
So, I'll just pop in with a quick reminder. You are okay! But
even if you were to be diagnosed with an anxiety disorder,
you'd be a part of a very large community. Anxiety disorders
are extremely common, affecting nearly a third of all adults
at some point in their lives.[3] That's a lot of people!

Some obvious questions come up after reading this statis-
tic: If anxiety disorders are so common, why is there such a
stigma of shame in the church surrounding feelings of fear?
Why are we so hesitant to tell others (especially our friends
who go to church with us and should want to help us) that

we are out here in the forest? Why are we so afraid to shout "Hello?" and hope someone who has been here before or who is out here with us comes to our rescue and reminds us that we are not alone?

I think, deep down, one of our biggest worries as Christian women is what our fear says about our faith. We think to ourselves, *If God tells me to fear not and if Jesus tells me He has given me His peace, yet I am still afraid, then what does that say about what I believe at my core?* So we worry. We worry because we deal with anxiety, and then we worry about what the anxiety says about who we are. On top of all that, we worry about what other people would say if they found out about our silent struggle.

And so, instead of feeling overwhelmed and crying out, "Help! I need help over here! Something's not right. I need my people to surround me!" shame keeps us silent. We wander through this darkness alone, willing ourselves to just *be* better.

The forest of fear can be one of the loneliest places for Christian women because only people who have made it out want to admit they are familiar with the woods of worry. Do you know what I mean? We hear things like, "Oh, I used to have anxiety." "I went through a season of anxiety." "I knew someone who faced anxiety, and then the Lord healed her." While those testimonies are tremendously life giving and it helps to know there are women who made it to the other side, what about a community for the women who are still walking through the dark? Why do we feel so much shame in admitting we haven't made it out of this place yet?

THOSE WHO STRUGGLE WITH ANXIETY HAVE A PROBLEM, BUT <u>THEY</u> ARE NOT THE PROBLEM.

I think we are hesitant to say we are anxious because for a very long time, the church has spoken from the position that anxiety is primarily a spiritual thought battle. When Christians struggle with fear, they are told, "Just pray more and read your Bible, and you'll have peace." And while it is true that anxiety can stem from an emotional trauma, a stressful life event, or a supernatural attack by the Enemy, anxiety can also be triggered by a broken process in the body. As a result, many churchgoing, Jesus-loving Christians with clinical anxiety wonder what's wrong with them and their faith. *I'm doing all that, and it's not changing anything. I must be the problem,* we believe. But that's a lie that must be addressed. Those who struggle with anxiety have a problem, but *they* are not the problem.

Have you ever done any research on what happens to people's bodies when they experience anxiety? It's really very interesting. Anxiety is one of the most common emotions across all species. It is the emotion that tells a living being to be on guard and aware of potential danger. Anxiety, at its core, helps keep us alive. Here's how.

When we stumble or get startled or sense immediate danger, our brains trigger a fight-or-flight response. Almost immediately, chemicals are released that prepare our bodies to face peril and fight it or run from it. This physiological response increases our alertness and causes us to pay very close attention to our surroundings. It makes us look for any possible threat. Our breathing changes, our bodies reroute blood, and our muscles are primed and ready to respond. It's why your heart races and you feel that rush of adrenaline when you nearly trip or the car in front of you brakes suddenly. Do you know that feeling?

This is all part of our bodies' autonomic nervous system, the system in charge of running things behind the scenes. This system is made up of two sets of nerves, the sympathetic and parasympathetic nervous systems.[4] I know this is getting really scientific, but stick with me for a second. There's a reason I'm telling you all this.

When our anxiety is triggered by some stimuli that says there is danger, the first system, the sympathetic nervous system, releases a round of chemicals that causes us to prepare for what we are about to face. The second system, the parasympathetic nervous system, acts like an antagonist, keeping the first system in check. In other words, the second system releases chemicals that act as a sort of antidote to the first.[5] It's all a careful dance of what we sense around us: how our brains interpret what we sense, how our brains then signal different response centers in our bodies, and how those systems function together to keep us from danger.

Why is it important that we understand how anxiety works? Because just like any other system, such as our immune, respiratory, circulatory, or digestive system, sometimes our nervous system has problems. Sometimes what's going on in our bodies affects our brains (which are also part of our bodies). And sometimes we need a doctor's input to aid what is wrong. I read recently in the book *The Struggle Is Real* that "about twenty percent of the population have one or more disorders related to brain chemistry that are primarily genetic."[6]

This is why you shouldn't be ashamed of admitting you are in the forest. Anxiety isn't your fault. It's not a result of fraudulent faith. You shouldn't be rejected religiously because of it. So, I'll repeat myself: Anxiety can stem from emotional trauma. It can be the result of a spiritual attack by the Enemy. Or it could be some form of physical brokenness, where a process in your body doesn't work the way it was designed to. There's much more to anxiety than many of us realize, and we must gain a fuller understanding of what we are dealing with if we are going to find hope and healing.

So, the first area where your heart might need healing is this: Perhaps you're afraid of feeling afraid. You wonder how you can call yourself a devoted follower of Christ when many days you've got an anxious heart and a racing mind. You wonder how you can point to Him as the answer for yourself and others when you've called on Him for peace but you still wake up afraid some days. You worry what the anxiety you feel says about who you are as a Christian woman. And you can't talk to others about it because the shame keeps you silent.

Before I say one more word, I want to make something abundantly clear. I want to say what pastors and other church leaders and kind church counselors should have told you a long time ago. I want to say what your heart has desperately needed to hear to begin to heal. Ready? Lean in.

ANXIETY DOES NOT DISQUALIFY YOU FROM BEING A WOMAN FULL OF FAITH.

Anxiety does not disqualify you from being a woman full of faith.

Full stop. Read it again. Underline it. Highlight it. It's true, and you're going to want to remember it. You might have been trained to believe that the anxiety you feel disqualifies you from being considered a faith-filled woman. You might have grown up doubting your relationship with Jesus, or you might have been told in your adult years that something is wrong with your relationship with Him because you feel afraid or have panic attacks. You might have been told this by people you trust in church leadership. But it's simply not true. You can *feel* afraid and *know* God is in control. You can *feel* anxious and *know* God is good. Because you are not what you feel, and sometimes our bodies don't line up with what our spirits know is true.

I'll give you an example. Just a few months ago, I was invited to minister at an event not far from my home in Los Angeles. I was part of the prayer team asked to simply pray during the weekend conference. I suppose you could think of my role that weekend as playing defense. While the speakers were on stage, the prayer team was praying against what the Enemy might try to do during the gathering. We were praying against distractions. We were praying against confusion. We were praying that the Lord would open hearts and minds and bring healing and inspiration to every person in attendance. We were praying that the conference speakers would say only what the Lord wanted them to share and that the attendees would fully receive the messages in such a way that the words transformed their hearts. I'm often the speaker at such events, so this was a new and exciting ministry opportunity for me.

It was the afternoon of the second day, and the team and I decided to get some coffee before the evening session. I don't drink coffee (a story I'll share later in the book), but I decided to go ahead and grab a dessert with the rest of the group. It was a nice afternoon, and I was really enjoying ministering as a team. But on our way back to the venue, my heart began to race. That familiar flush of anxiety raced through my body. I sat in the back seat, trying my hardest to make sense of what I was experiencing physically. *What's really going on?* I prayed. And immediately the Lord began to remind me about my day, bringing to my attention some simple facts. First, I hadn't gotten much sleep the night before because I was staying in a hotel. Second, I hadn't really eaten properly throughout the day because of the busy schedule. My body was reacting to physical stressors that I hadn't thought about until that moment. My heart was pounding. My hands were sweaty. My stomach hurt. My shoulders felt tense. Physically, I was on the verge of a panic attack, but it wasn't because I was weak in my faith. My body simply needed a good meal and the chance to pause and regroup.

So, here's the interesting part. During this short trip back to the conference venue, my spirit didn't feel overwhelmed at all. My physical heart was racing, but my spiritual heart was

looking forward to the evening service and what I antici-
pated God was about to do. This was the first time in my life
that I recognized a disconnect between what my body was
experiencing and what my heart was sensing spiritually. I
was full of faith, praying for the attendees of the conference
to encounter God's love in a new way, while at the same time,
my body wasn't behaving as it should.

PHYSICAL BROKENNESS DOES NOT LIMIT WHAT GOD DOES THROUGH US, NOR DOES IT ALTER HIS VIEW OF US AND OUR FAITH.

After about twenty minutes, my body came into align-
ment with my spirit—which sounds strange to say, but I just
mean my body stopped panicking and I began to physically
feel what my spirit had known all along. It was going to be a
great night, and I simply needed to eat something and rest
for a minute before I got back to work. That's exactly what
happened. I was able to fully step into what I had been asked
to do for the night. Anxiety didn't disqualify me from praying or ministering or sharing the love of Jesus any more than
deafness, diabetes, asthma, or any other chronic physical
disability might have. Do you know why? Physical brokenness does not limit what God does through us, nor does it
alter His view of us and our faith.

Jesus Only Uses Broken People

Sister, what you are is a spirit who lives in a body—a broken body. Your brokenness might look different from others'. Your brokenness might manifest mentally. Your brokenness might show up in your emotions. Your brokenness might be a result of some physical dysfunction that you have no control over. But make no mistake: You and I—and the rest of the entire world—live in broken flesh. The fact that we will all die proves this is true. Our brokenness just doesn't always look like everyone else's.

Remember, when God created humanity, He made us in His perfect image and designed us to live forever with Him in a garden made just for Him and His creation. Death was not part of the original plan. But when Adam and Eve sinned, God's children were separated from Him; death and brokenness entered their bodies *and minds*.

Yet God did not leave us in our brokenness. His plan was for us to be restored into right relationship with Him and into full wholeness. This rescue plan was carried out over thousands of years through God's imperfect people and ultimately through His perfect Son, Jesus. He gained the ultimate victory over death, but our days are still limited on earth. Brokenness still plagues our planet.

Every person—except for Jesus—whom God used to carry out His work on earth has been just as broken as you and me. Period. End of story. We are all broken folks used by God in some way to expand His kingdom and bring all the other broken folks back into a relationship with the Father.

Why is this important? Sister, your anxiety, your fear, your mind, your emotions, and the way your brokenness affects your life do not disqualify you from knowing, loving, and serving the Lord and from being used by Him. You and your heart and your life are a needed asset to the kingdom of God!

Feeling afraid doesn't disqualify you from being used by Jesus any more than chronic migraines or allergies to foods prevent one of our brothers or sisters from preaching the gospel of hope and healing. The fall of humankind at the beginning of time meant we would all be faulty on some level. It is the reason we all need Jesus.

GOD DOES NOT FAULT THE ANXIOUS WOMAN FOR HER ANXIETY. HE CAME SO THAT SHE—WE—COULD BE FREE!

So, let's exclaim this truth over the lie that says *we* are to blame for our anxiety. Ready?

God does not fault the anxious woman for her anxiety. He came so that she—we—could be free!

And whether that freedom comes by the vehicle of counseling, medication, vitamins, or an encounter with His presence that radically and miraculously reorganizes your DNA, my job is to walk with you, believing that hope and peace are coming for you. My job is to point to Jesus and say, "It's always been up to Him." Our job is to trust and follow Him and take every step He says to take.

We do not have to be afraid of feeling afraid. We do not have to fear the reality of being in the forest at night. God sent His Spirit and gave us His Word so that we could walk through this dark world with a lamp to our feet and a light to our path, and He gave us one another so we wouldn't have to walk this road alone. Sister, hold that lamp up a little higher because what you see here and whom you see in this space with you just might surprise you.

So many women are walking this journey with you, all realizing that none of us have to be afraid of the fear. There's hope in the Holy Spirit, who doesn't leave us. There's healing available as we acknowledge the many ways to become whole. And there's a host of other women all holding up their lights, all acknowledging that they aren't afraid of being afraid anymore, all making this dark forest a lot less scary, all on our walk toward healing.

Let's Pray Together

Father, You know exactly where the fear we face comes from. You know the root cause. Whether it's situational, relational, or physical, Lord, we ask that You'd help us now. Bring healing as only You can. Lead us as we take our next steps toward wholeness. We give our health journeys over to You. Help us know whom to talk to, where to seek treatment, which friends we can trust, and which methods we should explore.

We know that You are our healer. We know

that with just a word, You healed those in Scripture. With just a touch, others received full wholeness. So, right here, we ask that You'd touch us—minds, bodies, and spirits. Push back the darkness and bring complete healing. We trust You with our lives. We trust You with our hearts. We trust You to lead us. And we trust that You are good. Thank You for sending Jesus to make us whole. We ask in Jesus's name. Amen.

SAY THIS WITH ME

I'm not afraid of being afraid. The Lord doesn't fault me for the anxiety I face. He wants to free me. Therefore, I won't shame myself for needing His help!

TRY THIS

Grab your journal or open the notes application on your phone. After reading this first chapter, explain in your own words why anxiety does not disqualify you from being a woman full of faith.

2

Personalized Pathways to Peace

JESUS HEALS US USING MULTIPLE METHODS

He was sick. Really sick. Not just your average five-year-old-with-a-fever sick. My older son, Kolton, was suddenly fighting something much worse than I'd originally thought. The day before, he hadn't seemed to be suffering from anything more than a small cold. He had a runny nose and a little cough. I had kept him home from pre-K that morning not because he was too ill to learn but because I didn't want him to spread his virus to his classmates. But as the afternoon went on, I realized we were dealing with something much worse than the first-of-autumn sniffles. I made a call, and our family doctor was able to see him immediately. But Kolton seemed to become even worse on the way to his appointment. His chest hurt. He was gasping for breath. His doctor took one look at him and called immediately for transport to the Children's Hospital in Oklahoma City. At the time, we lived in northwest Oklahoma, and the nearest children's hospital was two hours away. The entire ambulance ride I prayed they would be able find out what was really going on with my little boy.

When we got to the ER, the scene unfolded as you might expect. His gurney was wheeled into an exam room, where doctors and nurses rushed in to begin performing tests. They took X-rays and drew blood. They performed an ultrasound and gave him a full examination. But nothing seemed to indicate he was experiencing anything more than a vicious virus. Hours later, my husband and I were told he should feel better with some rest and rehydration. They gave him medicine to reduce his high fever, and they told us to take him home. We were instructed to bring him back if anything changed.

Reluctantly, we left the hospital. Sometimes as mommas, we just know when things aren't right, and in this case, I was not convinced Kolton was fighting a simple virus. He seemed so sick. I just didn't know what else it could be.

We decided to stay at my mom's house that night. She lived near the hospital, and if anything were to change in Kolton's condition, I wanted to get him back to the professionals as quickly as possible. I didn't want to have to worry about being two hours away from the people who were trained to help him. I can't tell you how glad I was we made that decision when I went in to check on him in the middle of the night and found that his fever had spiked to 105 degrees. He was dazed. He was shaking. He was struggling to take full breaths.

In a panic, my husband and I raced him back to the hospital, where the staff all agreed we had made the right decision to return. They drew more blood. They took additional images of his abdomen and chest, and they soon discovered what my mommy sense knew all along. Kolton wasn't just fighting off a cold after all. He had a severe case of pneumonia that was hidden behind his heart. The first radiologist had missed it, but in the middle of the night, a second radiologist recognized what was actually going on in his body. Once Kolton had been properly diagnosed, they admitted him for treatment. The doctors just had to find the cause of his sickness so he could improve. It took a specialized plan and course of medicine for him to leave the hospital a few days later, this time on a path to complete health.

You know, so often those of us with anxiety are just like my son. We know something's wrong. We can tell we aren't well, but we aren't sure what the underlying cause of it is. Maybe you are receiving treatment, friend. Maybe you have a plan in place and a great team that surrounds you and supports you, but chances are you don't. I say that because only a little over 35 percent of those with an anxiety disorder actually receive treatment.[1] That means about two-thirds of us don't. We just hope to get better on our own. The reality is, if we are going to find hope and healing, we might need a second round of professionals to take another look.

The First Round of Help

For most of us Christian women, the first people we seek counsel from concerning the anxiety we face are those who help us spiritually. Would you say that's accurate? Maybe you've never sat down to talk about it with your pastor or another church leader, but you have likely received your pastor's advice, whether or not they knew they were speaking to you. You have probably attended a church service or read a book or listened to a podcast from someone you trust where a link between faith and fear was discussed. I think we all have. With faith being such a central theme in our Christian lives, most of us have been taught that to decrease the fear in our lives, we should increase our prayer time, focus on what God says in His Word, and elevate the intensity of our worship. That is the standard treatment plan.

Honestly, this is all great advice when it comes to the spiritual aspects of anxiety. They really are solid suggestions. However, anxiety isn't only a spiritual thought battle. Sometimes, as in my son's situation, the actual issue is buried underneath what seems to be so simple on the surface. And sometimes, without even realizing it, spiritual professionals (pastors, teachers, church leaders) send us home to take care of the anxiety on our own, when what we really need is a second opinion from a doctor, geneticist, or counselor to get to the root of it.

Now, just to be clear, these church leaders in our lives don't always realize they are "sending us home." Do you know what I mean? As they teach about faith and give us spiritual strategies, they are speaking from their area of expertise. They are addressing an important part of anxiety, one that we will address later in the book. But in these faith-centered messages, church leaders don't always consider us. By that I mean their messages aren't focused on the mommas in the room who are doing everything they're suggesting but with no success. So, we shouldn't fault faith leaders for not addressing potential underlying causes of our anxiety. Right? But that doesn't mean we haven't been hurt at some point by those who seem to be telling us that overcoming fear is simple for dedicated believers.

I need to ask you something, and I want you to be honest with your answer. Okay? Do you feel as though other Christians (both in leadership and in social settings) have been understanding and compassionate when discussing faith, fear, and feelings of anxiety? I sincerely hope this is the case for you. I hope you have found a safe place to walk out your journey of health and wholeness, supported by those whom God calls to be lights in the darkness. But I don't think it would be right to ignore the fact that maybe your experience has been different. Perhaps you went to church or chatted with other people who love Jesus, and rather than finding hope in the dark, you left feeling even more alone.

Perhaps like my son's first trip to the children's hospital, you were assessed by those in church leadership and told if you just addressed your heart issues or some secret sin or some failure of your belief, you'd feel better. Perhaps without any deeper evaluation of your condition, you were sent away with the directions to simply "try harder."

Friend, if that's been a part of your story, I can't move on without saying I'm sorry. I'm sorry you felt sent home. I'm sorry you didn't feel heard. I'm sorry people who represent the Lord didn't understand or get it right in the way they responded to you or tried to help you. I'm sorry you heard messages from leaders that made you feel as if something were wrong with your faith, when the fear was actually caused by an underlying condition that had nothing to do with what you believe.

I'm sorry others were not always encouraging, even when they meant well and even when they were addressing a part of the problem. I'm sorry others hurt you, even when they were trying to help you. And I'm sorry you did not receive the help you needed when you bravely shouted "Helloooo?" into the dark night, hoping someone would come to your rescue and lead you out of the fear. Ultimately, I'm sorry a stigma still surrounds mental illness among Christians.

I recognize this might not have been your experience. You might be reading this and thinking, *I have found only hope and support from my brothers and sisters in Christ.* For that, we should pause and thank the Lord for the times His church loves as it should. I know that each of our journeys with anxiety is unique, but for some of us, finding healing means stopping to address what has hurt us. And if you have been wounded by those who love Jesus, I want to remind you that God isn't always perfectly represented by His people.

God doesn't place blame or shame on you. He isn't sitting in heaven with His arms crossed, saying, *Well, if she just believed Me more, she'd be better.* No, sis. God is with you right now as you read these words, and every thought He has about you is filtered through His love. When He looks at you, He doesn't see disappointment. He sees His daughter. He doesn't see lacking faith. He sees the price Jesus paid for your emotional freedom. He doesn't see a hopeless case. He sees every step you are going to take together to become whole.

GOD KNOWS HOW BRAVE YOU REALLY ARE.

And whether or not His church always understands your circumstances, God knows how brave you really are. He knows how strong you try to be for your family. And He knows just how exhausted you feel from always trying to be so strong and brave.

So, can we pause here for just a second to imagine God as the kind papa He really is? He's not mad. He's not shaking His head in disappointment. Picture Him along with me. He's there in the room with you right now. His face is full of compassion. His arms are extended, and He's inviting you into His love. He wants to hold you, and as you lean against His chest and feel His heartbeat, He puts His face down into your hair and whispers, *I know, sweetheart. I know. It's okay. I've got you. I know they didn't always understand, but I do.*

Take a deep breath with me for just a minute.

GOD HAS A STRATEGY TO BRING YOU HEALING, FRIEND, AND IT IS TAILOR MADE AND DYED RED WITH HIS BLOOD.

Sister, it is of vital importance that you see the Lord from this perspective as He walks with you toward wholeness. He loves you. He's on your side. He sees what is going on be-neath the surface, and together you're going to get to the root of it. Together you're going to take a second look and bring to the surface what's really going on in your mind, body, and spirit. He has a personalized pathway to lead you to peace. God has a strategy to bring you healing, friend, and it is tailor made and dyed red with His blood.

Solutions for Sight

So, here's the deal. If the anxiety you face isn't a simple lack of faith—if there is truly some underlying condition—then healing for you might look different than healing for me. I wish it were as simple as this: We need A. God does B. The results are always C. The truth is, God often uses multiple methods to bring about the same results and always in His timing. We see this evidenced throughout the Bible.

Let's talk for just a second about the blind men Jesus healed in Scripture. The men Jesus healed in Matthew 20 cried out for Jesus to have mercy on them, and He asked, "What do you want me to do for you?"[2] Jesus touched their eyes, and they received their sight. That's how these men were healed. But another man is mentioned in John 9. This man became the center of discussion as people asked Jesus whose sin had caused his blindness. Jesus said this man was blind "so that the works of God might be displayed in him."[3] Then Jesus spit on the ground and made mud with His saliva. He anointed the man's eyes with the mud and said to him, "Go . . . wash in the Pool of Siloam."[4] So he went and washed and came back seeing.

In both stories, the men received their sight. All the men were healed by Jesus. They all had an encounter with the living God. Yet the Lord healed these men in individual ways because He knew best. The same is true when it comes to the ways God heals us. Jesus is always the answer, but He uses multiple methods to bring about our wholeness.

Let me say that again, just so we are clear. Jesus is our healer. Jesus is the hope we need. He has already overcome hell and the grave. He paid the price for our healing. But just as He sent one blind man to wash in the pool and touched other blind men so they'd receive their sight, Jesus might heal you differently than He heals me. For some, healing might come with just a touch. For others, He might use doctors and therapists and counselors and pastors and others who will be instrumental in their process to wholeness.

The good news is Jesus still heals today. He has a miracle waiting for each of us. We just might need to reevaluate what we consider miraculous.

What Is Miraculous?

The first recorded miracle of Jesus took place at a wedding where He and His disciples were guests. When the wine ran out, Jesus's mother, Mary, who was there as well, came to

Jesus and said, "They have no more wine."[5] After Jesus reminded her that His time had not yet come (basically, *Mom!
It's not time for Me to do this stuff yet!*), she looked at the servants and told them to do whatever Jesus instructed. So they
did. There were large jars used for ceremonial washing, and
Jesus instructed the servants to fill them with water and
present some to the master of the banquet. When they did
as Jesus directed, the water turned into the finest wine.

Before Jesus brought sight to the blind, healed lepers,
raised the dead, cast out demons, forgave sins, or strength-
ened legs to walk, He turned water into wine. I think it's interesting that Scripture says, "What Jesus did here in Cana
of Galilee was the first of the signs through which he revealed his glory; and his disciples believed in him."[6] Why do
I think this is interesting? Because this miracle was momen-
tary, yet its effects were eternal.

Scripture doesn't say what happened to all that wine. My
guess is as good as yours. I'm assuming the guests drank it
and sometime shortly after the wedding, it was all gone.
(That was the whole reason Mary prompted Jesus to perform this miraculous act in the first place.)

Do you know what didn't happen in this story? Jesus
didn't make jars of never-ending wine. You can't go to Galilee
and drink from these jars today. Jesus performed the miracle,
and the wine was drunk. The fact that the wine didn't last
forever doesn't make this story any less miraculous. Would
you agree? Would you agree that the miracle is still awesome
even though the wine eventually ran out?

I can think of quite a few other times in Scripture when

God performed miracles that we might consider temporary. How about the time when Jesus fed more than four thousand people or the time when He fed more than five thousand? Jesus miraculously multiplied a little bit of bread and fish and fed thousands upon thousands of people. Everyone had her fill, and baskets of food were even left over.[7] But we can't eat some of that bread and fish today. It didn't become an all-you-can-eat buffet for the rest of eternity. Scripture speaks about a heavenly banquet, but this wasn't it. This was a miraculous moment.

What about when Jesus calmed the storm? He spoke to the wind and waves, and they obeyed.[8] But there have been storms on the Sea of Galilee since, right? (The answer is actually easy because the way the mountain air and the humid air over the water interact sets the stage for sudden storms.) Jesus didn't calm the air over the Sea of Galilee forever and declare it a no-storm zone. He calmed the storm, but later more storms occurred.

Or what about Lazarus, Jesus's friend who died but whom Jesus miraculously resurrected? Lazarus had been in the tomb for four days when Jesus called him out, and he lived again![9] It was a miracle! But if you go to Bethany today, Lazarus isn't there. He eventually died . . . again.

The wine was consumed, the bread was eaten, storms over the Sea of Galilee still occur, and Lazarus is now dead. Yet each one of those events was a miraculous display of God's divine wonder! Each one revealed His glory and the awesomeness of His power, compassion, and love. Make no mistake: God was a miracle maker then and is still a miracle maker today. But what if we discredited these miracles because they lasted only a moment? What if we were less impressed because they weren't permanent? It would seem a little silly, don't you suppose?

My point is this: Could you perhaps have overlooked some miracles God has performed in your life because they lasted only a moment? Maybe God miraculously provided for you financially, but you needed Him to provide again when more unexpected bills arrived. Or maybe He resurrected a dead friendship, but He needed to bring healing to other places of pain or disagreement. Or maybe, just maybe, He brought you supernatural peace in the middle of fear, but the next day you needed Him to calm your anxious heart again.

MIRACULOUS MOMENTS ARE STILL MIRACLES!

As we contend for complete healing from anxiety, we must pay attention to the moment-by-moment divine intervention in our lives. Miraculous moments are still miracles! Would you agree? Do you consider it a miracle when you go into a situation that would normally trigger a panic attack and do not experience one? Do you consider it a miracle when you find yourself breathing easily, your shoulders are relaxed, and you have no tension in your body, when everything about your day would ordinarily steal your physical peace? Do you consider it a miracle when you are able to rest at the end of the day rather than feel your mind spinning out? These are all miraculous moments, revealing God's hand at work in your life. But often as we pray and ask God for total healing, we overlook the daily proof of His power.

Sister, I'm not asking you to limit your view of what God can do. Just the opposite! I'm asking you to expand your view of God's miraculous intervention in your life. Sometimes we are like the Israelites, God's chosen people who were promised land flowing with milk and honey. God led them out of slavery in Egypt, parted the Red Sea, provided bread from heaven as food in the wilderness, supplied water from a rock when they were thirsty, gave them a strategy to overcome the people inhabiting their promised land, and continuously met their needs. Yet God's people often doubted His goodness and questioned His power. They grumbled, saying, "If only we had died in Egypt, or even here in the wilderness!"[10]

Hadn't they witnessed God's love and provision over and over? Was any part of it less miraculous simply because they still needed God to lead them and provide for them daily? You and I know the answer. And while it's not fun to be compared to the Israelites in this story (sorry!), we should learn from them and begin to look for evidence of God's love and power in our own lives.

EVERY MOMENT WHEN YOU AND I OVERCOME ANXIETY, WE ARE LIVING A MIRACLE!

Are we not experiencing the miraculous power of God as He brings peace to our hearts and minds daily? Are we not living miracles when we are able to easily do what would cripple us in fear some days? The truth is, every moment when you and I overcome anxiety, we are living a miracle! Every moment when we have peace and balanced hearts, we are reminded of the continual presence and love of Jesus for us. If you wake up one morning with supernatural peace, do not overlook it. Don't say, "But tomorrow I might be anxious again." No! You should praise God for the miracle of your peace and acknowledge that all God's people need Him to provide for them each day. The Word says His mercies are new every morning.[11]

The fact that you might wake up tomorrow and need God again doesn't mean you didn't experience His miracle-working power today. It means He is still God and you are still walking through a broken world in need of His presence.

Let's pause for just a minute and consider this. The God who loves you knows every part of you. He knows exactly how your brain works. He knows how your body works. He knows what you've been through. He knows how hard it has been. He knows how desperate you've felt. He knows how much you crave rest. He knows just how much you want to be healed, and through His sacrifice, He made a way for you to be whole.

Today, let's lean into His love. Let's look for the daily miracles and displays of His goodness and power. Let's ask the Lord to help us get to the root of the fear, and let's take His hand as His presence leads us down personalized pathways to peace.

LET'S PRAY TOGETHER

....

Father, thank You for not sending us away to deal with the anxiety we face on our own. Thank You for being the God who heals. Thank You for knowing every step we will take and every strategy we will use to overcome anxiety.

Our healing was made possible by the work of Your Son on the cross. Our hope is found in Him. No matter what steps You invite us to take, help us remember that You are the one who heals us. You are the one who brings life. You are the one who has a plan for us.

We ask that You'd help us get to the root of the anxiety we face. Help us find the right doctors, counselors, and resources to aid us on our healing journey. Help us address all aspects of anxiety, including both spiritual and physical. You are the God of peace, and we thank You for each miraculous moment when we overcome fear. We ask in Jesus's name. Amen.

SAY THIS WITH ME

....

Jesus made healing available to me! I don't fault myself for experiencing anxiety, and I believe that Jesus is leading me out of it! Each day I overcome fear is a miracle, so I will praise the Lord for His love and healing power in my life.

TRY THIS

....

Make a list of the methods that God has used to bring healing to your mental health in the past. Did He lead you to counseling? A doctor? A change in your diet? As you review, pause to consider the miraculous moments you may have previously overlooked.

3

Lions, Tigers, and a Million Modern Fears (Oh My!)

How Modern Motherhood Affects Our Mental Health

The conversation with my mom went something like this: "Okay, Mom, I need you to pull this rocking chair up to Kolton's crib and watch him while he sleeps."

My mom looked at me, doing her best not to seem as though she thought my request was strange. "Sure. No problem. All night?"

An unspoken conversation was happening in this moment that my momma knew I wasn't quite ready to have out loud. Were either of us going to acknowledge that I was crossing the line from rational to irrational fear?

It was the second night home from the hospital with our firstborn, and I was not in a good headspace. My mom was there helping and was trying to figure out whether I was really asking her to stay awake all night long and make sure Kolton kept breathing. That was exactly what I was asking her to do. Deep down she knew it, and so did I. She saw that I was overly anxious, and she understood. She suffers from her own anxiety disorder and knew this would bring me a level of peace that night. She was just trying to help her own child work through these first days of new motherhood. So she smiled and promised that she'd keep watch over Kolton until the sun rose the next morning.

I was a scared little momma. I know there are likely very few women who truly felt confident in their parenting from the day they first held their little ones in their arms. After all, babies require us to make a million decisions we have no expertise in, and we all hope our children don't suffer the consequences of our making the wrong ones. But even so, there is a difference between new moms just doing their very best to figure it all out and new moms who cannot complete normal daily activities because they are consumed by postpartum anxiety (PPA). I fell into the second group.

Yep. I lived through postpartum anxiety with all three of my children, but I didn't realize it until much later. Constant fear and dread overwhelmed my thinking. I couldn't sleep. I never had peace. I adopted rituals that eased my troubled mind, but I rarely rested in my mothering. I was a mess and needed help, but I didn't know it. No one around me recognized how far the intrusive tentacles of fear reached inside me either, even though they were there from the beginning.

The intense anxiety, worse than the day-to-day anxiety I had lived with up until that point, surfaced the first night I brought Kolton home from the hospital. I can't remember walking into the house, but I can remember sitting on the couch, holding him in my arms, and wondering if I could ever put him down again.

In fairness, Kolton had a few medical issues that made

laying him down in his crib and walking into the other room more difficult than for your average newborn. He had terrible acid reflux, so whenever we put him on his back, stomach acid would come up and burn his esophagus. He'd scream mercilessly and stop only when I picked him up and nursed him to relieve the pain.

On top of that, Kolton also was born just a little early and did something called periodic breathing. He'd breathe rapidly for a few seconds and then hold his breath for up to ten. Then he'd repeat. According to his pediatrician, his respiratory system was regulating his carbon dioxide and oxygen levels. Whereas our adult bodies—and most babies'—do this with each inhale and exhale, his system was still figuring it all out. He would breathe quickly, taking in a lot of oxygen, and then hold his breath while the levels fell. Then his brain would trigger him to do it again. But I will tell you right now that as a new mom with anxiety, watching my infant hold his breath for ten seconds felt like an eternity.

The compulsion to hold and watch Kolton was excessive. What if he never started breathing again? What if he just held his breath forever and went blue? I had read so many tragic reports about babies who passed away from sudden infant death syndrome (SIDS), even though the heartbroken parents had done everything right. I was absolutely convinced something terrible could happen to my baby if I took my eyes off him for even just a moment.

After hours and hours of labor and then adjusting to nursing every few hours, I was emotionally and physically exhausted. I didn't know what to do. In my overwhelmingly anxious state as a brand-new, terribly sleep-deprived parent,

I decided I'd have to stay awake for all eternity or find someone who could hold or watch Kolton while he slept. So that's
exactly what I did. I asked my mom, who was staying with
us for those first few days, if she'd stay awake and make sure
Kolton was okay. I am not kidding. This was my solution.
Obviously, this was a terrible idea. But anxiety said, *You have
no other options. Either you hold him or watch him, or he could
die.* And I agreed.

In between feedings, my mom took Kolton into the other
room and held him while I rested for a few hours. When
Kolton started to fuss, my momma came into my room and
placed him in my arms. I held him to my chest and groggily
fed him.

My mind whirred. I was trying to figure out a system for
the three of us (my mom, my husband, and me), where we
could rotate nights and watch Kolton through the midnight
hours. That was just about the time that Jared rolled over
and asked, "What are you holding?" I was devastated. This
was my backup. This guy was the one who was going to
make sure Kolton breathed successfully until dawn.

I nervously laughed and answered, "A baby."

Terribly confused, he asked, "Whose baby?!" I knew right
then that unless my momma was around, it would be up to
me to manage all night shifts from then on.

With this, I panicked even more. Kolton wasn't even a
week old, and I already recognized how wholly exhausted I
was. How on earth was I going to keep watch over this baby
for the rest of his life?

They tell the momma to sleep when the baby sleeps, but I
couldn't. I would stare at Kolton and ensure he was breath-

ing. I was the mom who held her finger under her sleeping child's nose a few dozen times a day to make sure he was still inhaling and exhaling. I was the mom who was afraid to drive more than ten minutes because what if my baby's neck was positioned in such a way that his airway was blocked? I was the mom who wondered how I'd ever get anything done if all I could do was watch my child sleep. And I was the momma who cried when everyone went home and back to work and it was entirely up to me to keep guard. I didn't cry because I was depressed. I sobbed because I was anxiously shattered and emotionally exhausted.

Looking back, I have a clearer perspective. I can *see* the factors that led to my fear. Actual medical issues contributed to the situation. I can *sympathize* with that precious momma who was just doing her best. Bless her heart, she loved her baby so much that she gave up every basic need of her own to care for him. But I can also *understand* now just how unhealthy I was, mentally and emotionally.

You know, at the time, my fear seemed rational to me. It seemed like a good, safe, typical response. I see now just how much help I really needed. I wish I had called out into that dark night, "Helloooo!? Is anyone there? Can anyone help me?" I wish I had told someone just how afraid I was every single day, and I wish I had seen a doctor about it. Physical stress and lack of sleep can contribute to a person's anxiety, and I was stuck in a cycle where my fear kept me awake and then lack of proper rest caused the anxiety to grow. It was relentless.

Friend, there is a place where the stress and worry begin

to take a physical toll on the momma and her baby, and help is important. So, I want to say two things here. First, if you lived through postpartum anxiety, whether or not you recognized it in the moment, give yourself some grace. Don't shame the new momma you were. Don't laugh at her fear because you know so much better now. Look back and see exactly where Jesus stood as you paced the nursery during those nights. Ask Him to show you how He sat with you as you kept vigilant watch. How He spoke kindly to you as you did your very best when you felt as though you were at the end of yourself. And then ask Him to bring healing to your memories of those heavy days. It was a time when He held you so closely, so much more than you might have realized. Because while the fear was loud, the Lord was ever present, strengthening you in your weakness and proving Himself strong.

Next, if you are a momma of a new baby and you relate to my story at all, tell someone. Some studies suggest that as many as 10 percent of mothers experience some degree of postpartum anxiety. I'm not a doctor, but according to postpartum.net, here are some common signs and symptoms:

+ constant worry
+ feeling that something bad is going to happen
+ racing thoughts
+ disturbances of sleep and appetite
+ inability to sit still
+ physical symptoms like dizziness, hot flashes, and nausea[1]

If you're in a place where these thoughts or behaviors are interfering with your daily life, reach out. Call your friend or mom or sister. Reach out to your OB or midwife. Find a licensed therapist or counselor. Contact the American Association of Christian Counselors (aacc.net or 1-800-526-8673). Talk to other moms. Take practical steps, such as saying to someone you trust, "I need help. Can you sit with my baby while I take a nap? Can you care for my other children while I take care of my baby? Can you bring me a meal? Can you listen while I tell you how I'm feeling?" Mommas who are facing debilitating anxiety often stay silent. Whether they don't realize they are experiencing PPA or are embarrassed about it, too often moms do not seek help. But you are not weak in telling someone you aren't okay. You show strength when you acknowledge, "I need help, maybe even even professional or medical help, to make it through this."

YOU ARE NOT WEAK IN TELLING SOMEONE YOU AREN'T OKAY.

Can you get to the other side of this on your own? Probably. But you shouldn't have to, sis. The Lord shows us throughout Scripture how important it is for us to lean on others when we are vulnerable. Consider what Solomon (a man of profound wisdom) said in Ecclesiastes 4:10: "If one person falls, the other can reach out and help. But someone who falls alone is in real trouble."[2]

Whereas the Enemy of our hearts wants us to struggle alone, the Lord wants to lead us to people who can represent

His arms holding us up, His hands helping us, and His love carrying us through our darkest and most overwhelming moments.

Finally, friend, if you are years or maybe even decades past the new-baby phase and you still face daily crippling fear, it's not too late to say you're struggling too. Today is a very good day to ask the Lord exactly where you should go or whom you should reach out to for help. He and I will be so proud of you for refusing to stay silent any longer. Pause and whisper this prayer right now: *Lord, what do You want me to do next to get the help my heart needs so I can have peace? Settle around me with Your love and healing as You direct my next steps. I ask in Jesus's name. Amen.*

Modern-Day Mothering

Though my children have grown and my postpartum anxiety has passed, the world still seems so unsafe. The list of fears, concerns, and areas where I need to be on my guard appears to grow with my kids. Yet I can't help but wonder if the world really is more dangerous today than it was ten years ago. Don't get me wrong. I fully understand that the modern threat of the internet and handheld devices is something previous generations didn't face. I get it. But those generations had other threats that modern advances in science and medicine have made nearly obsolete today. We've just exchanged their threats for ours.

One thing I believe today's parents deal with more than

other generations did, however, is the level of available information. Here's an example. A few years ago, I was in the nursery rocking one of my small children as he fell asleep for the night, and I scrolled through Facebook on my phone. I passed photos and status updates, and then I came across a viral article shared by multiple friends about a dad who found out that his teenage daughter had been the victim of an internet predator. He had so many fail-safes in place. He'd checked off so many boxes on the well-known but unwritten safety sheet concerning smart devices and teenagers.

He'd monitored his daughter's phone closely. He'd put restrictions on the hours she could be on it. He knew all her friends and most of their parents. He'd chosen not to allow her to use certain applications that could compromise her safety. He was an involved, observant father, but smartphones are called smart for a reason. A sneaky app developer had created a program that could be used for contacting friends and was masked as another kind of app so it could be hidden from parents. This man's daughter had used this dangerous program to meet a man pretending to be a teenager. The story didn't end well.

THE EASILY ACCESSIBLE INFORMATION ABOUT FUTURE POTENTIAL THREATS STEALS PRESENT PEACE.

This dad seemed to have done everything right to protect his child, yet he was unable to keep her from harm. My heart ached for him and for what his story could mean for parents everywhere. *Could this happen to me? To my children?* I found myself thinking about how I was going to keep my kids safe from such a real modern-day threat. I wondered, *What boundaries do I need to put in place? What strategies do I need to come up with before my children reach that age? What else do I need to worry about? What am I missing?*

I was rocking a child nearly a decade away from these possible dangers, but I had pulled myself into that moment. This is one reason today's parents are so anxious. The easily accessible information about future potential threats steals present peace.

Online discussion boards, social media groups, and parents' interconnectivity through their smart devices prove that we have more access to information (professional and amateur) than any generation before us. While this seems good, it is a direct threat to our peace. We are continually reminded of how much we have to fear. Have you noticed this? Every choice has a best option, and around every corner is a danger we haven't even considered. At least that's the way it feels. Today's parenting choir isn't going to let us miss any possible worst-case scenario our children might one day face or let us forget the terrible things that could happen if we get something wrong. We've all heard our share of these: "Don't choose the wrong way to feed your baby, the wrong diapers, the wrong sleep position, the wrong soaps, the wrong day care. Watch out for the wrong amount of screen time, the wrong car seats, the wrong vaccines, the wrong schools, the wrong friends, the wrong way to do bedtime. Be sure not to choose the wrong medicines, the wrong discipline, the wrong affirmations, or the wrong way to show love." We have endless access to encyclopedias of facts and opinions, and we have been made to feel as though our kids cannot afford for us to make any incorrect choices. We feel we must pay attention and get it all right or our children will face the terrible consequences of our ignorance.

The only problem is, no matter what you choose, some group is telling you you're making the wrong choice. You're making the wrong choice if you breastfeed or bottle-feed. Or if you choose to homeschool your children or send them to public or private school. If you go to work, you're neglecting your children. If you stay at home, you're not showing them that women are strong and can provide. You're making the wrong choice if you wear your baby or if you let him cry it out. There's a wrong choice whether or not you vaccinate or whether or not you choose to give your children cell phones. I'm not saying I believe that right or wrong decisions exist here. I'm simply saying that no matter the choice you make in any area, entire groups of mothers will be waiting to tell you why you are wrong.

THE WORST DANGER MIGHT JUST BE WHAT THIS DEAFENING DIN OF POTENTIAL DOOM IS DOING TO THE HEARTS OF TODAY'S MOMMAS.

No wonder we are anxious! The dangers today might not be any more *dangerous* than they were a century ago, but they are hands down a hundred times louder. This is the real threat to modern motherhood. Have you stopped to consider that? The worst threat to modern motherhood might not be anything our children face. The worst danger might just be what this deafening din of potential doom is doing to the hearts of today's mommas.

In our quest to make sure nothing bad ever happens to our kids, something truly tragic has happened to us. We have sacrificed our emotional and mental well-being on the altar of protecting our children. Fear has convinced us to pay close attention to everything it warns of, and we are worrying ourselves sick because of it.

I can't help but think of the Venus flytrap. This plant secretes a nectar to attract its prey. When a fly or other insect lands on it, the plant triggers a springlike response and the bug finds itself locked in the jaws of the carnivorous plant. What does this have to do with us? As vigilant moms, we seek out information, hoping to use it to protect our children. But just like the fly is drawn to the sweetness of the Venus flytrap, we are lured by information and soon discover that we are locked in fear's grip.

We hear that knowledge is power, and it's true. But information in fear's hands is dangerous. I once saw a quote posted online by *Good Housekeeping* that said, "It's like no one in my family appreciates that I stayed up all night overthinking for them."[3] We are losing sleep at night, rest in our days, and peace in our spirits all in the name of being good parents. And it's causing us harm.

Momma, we both know that the Word tells us no one gains anything by worrying. You know you won't add to your

children's lives by worrying whether they're going to be okay.
Jesus reminded us this is true in Matthew 6:27: "Can any one
of you by worrying add a single hour to your life?" But,
friend, we can add vibrantly to our kids' lives by praying for
each of their days and inviting the Lord to come close and
help us with each one.

> # WE MUST BE EQUALLY VIGILANT ABOUT PROTECTING OUR HEARTS FROM FEAR AS WE ARE ABOUT PROTECTING OUR CHILDREN FROM DANGER.

Am I saying to stop paying attention to your instincts? To
stop looking out for your kids' best interests? To be okay
with whatever might happen? Absolutely not. I am *not* saying that at all. I am saying we must be equally vigilant about
protecting our hearts from fear as we are about protecting
our children from danger. And as women who struggle with
anxiety, maybe we need to put some boundaries in place to
protect our peace. Maybe we limit our time on social media.
Maybe we pray after reading each story, inviting the Holy
Spirit to help us take the information and leave the fear.
Maybe we ask the Lord to help us recognize when we are
being affected negatively by what we are consuming so we
can press pause on the peace-poaching posts and consume
more of His truth instead. And maybe being vigilant means
holding each potential danger up to the cross and saying,

That is where Jesus said I could trust Him. He will protect me, and He will help me protect my kids.

While the threats are real, so is our God. And He has not forfeited His ability to care for us or our children because we suddenly recognize what He has known all along. The world is dangerous, but He remains on the throne.

Brave Momma

A few years ago, I heard a story about a momma who saved her baby during a tornado.[4] Without much warning, she discovered the storm would pass directly over her and her infant child. She didn't have time to seek shelter, but thinking quickly, she strapped her baby into an infant carrier and looped her arm through the handle. Within minutes the tornado ripped through her home, lifting her and her baby into the air and throwing them violently. Both miraculously survived. When asked later about her experience, the momma said she just knew she couldn't let go. "I was afraid if I let go, it [the tornado] was going to take her and I'd never find her."

I cried when I heard what this brave woman had done. It was such a pure picture of a mother's sacrificial love. Stories like hers always make me emotional. Do they have the same effect on you? I've read about mothers fighting off polar bears, lifting cars off their trapped children, or prying open the jaws of a crocodile to save their kids. They are moms just like the rest of us who would do anything to rescue their children from harm. We might not have personally faced situations like theirs, but this kind of love is in all of us. Mothers are nurturing protectors who would lay down their lives without hesitation for their children.

But can I repaint these stories for just a moment? Because when we hear about moms braving the odds, taking on attackers bigger than themselves, or defying logical strength to rescue their kids from overturned vehicles or wild animals, we sometimes forget they weren't alone. We forget that God wraps His arms around ours as we protect our kids.

Can you imagine the Lord being there with that momma as the tornado came close? Just as that sweet mom was flying through the air, arms clutched around the infant carrier, God was holding her just as tightly. Or the momma who pulled open the crocodile's powerful jaws? Can you see Him strengthening her arms, giving her the power to do the impossible? I know adrenaline plays a part in the ability to perform acts of unusual strength. I know that these women might not have been followers of Jesus, so I'm not saying they invited Him to intervene during their moments of desperation. But I am saying that when we look at their stories, we see where the Lord might stand in ours.

YOU ARE A BRAVE MOM, BUT IT'S NOT JUST UP TO YOU TO KEEP YOUR KIDS SAFE.

Here is some truth you need to hear: you are a brave mom, but it's not just up to you to keep your kids safe. Stop. Pause. Say it out loud: "It's not just up to me to protect my children."

When God placed children in your arms, He wasn't testing you to see how well you'd do on your own. Father God didn't say, *Wonder how this is going to go! Hey, Jesus, let's watch. This should be good!* No! The opposite happened. When God made you a parent, He placed within you not just the ability to care for your children but also the ability to call on Him to help you care for them—to borrow His strength, His wisdom, and His peace and to call on His Holy Spirit to guide you.

God looked across the earth before the beginning of time and chose to place your children into your care, fully intending for you to seek His counsel, invite Him into your everyday situations, and involve Him in each aspect of raising those babies. Then, like any kind father, He continued to keep careful watch, intimately involved in all your days. You may feel as though you're the only one standing there as the shield between your children and the world, but it's an incorrect picture. The Word tells us the truth. Just listen to what Psalm 91 says. Slowly read it like a promise from the one who cannot break His word. And make it personal: wherever you see a blank, insert your children's names.

Those who live in the shelter of the Most High
will find rest in the shadow of the Almighty.

This I declare about the LORD:
He alone is my refuge, my place of safety;
    he is my God, and I trust him.
For he will rescue _____ from every trap
    and protect [them] from deadly disease.
He will cover _____ with his feathers.
    He will shelter [them] with his wings.
    His faithful promises are [their] armor and protec-
      tion.
Do not be afraid of the terrors of the night,
    nor the arrow that flies in the day.
Do not dread the disease that stalks in darkness,
    nor the disaster that strikes at midday.
Though a thousand fall at [their] side,
    though ten thousand are dying around _____,
    these evils will not touch [them].
Just open your eyes,
    and see how the wicked are punished.

If _____ make the LORD [their] refuge,
    if _____ make the Most High [their] shelter,
no evil will conquer [them];
    no plague will come near your home.
For he will order his angels
    to protect _____ wherever [they] go.
They will hold _____ up with their hands
    so [they] won't even hurt [their] foot on a stone.
_____ will trample upon lions and cobras;
    _____ will crush fierce lions and serpents under
      [their] feet!

The LORD says, "I will rescue those who love me.
  I will protect those who trust in my name.
When _____ call on me, I will answer;
  I will be with them in trouble.
  I will rescue and honor them.
I will reward them with a long life
  and give them my salvation."⁵

Did you put in your kids' names as you read? I hope so. I hope you made it a declaration that produced peace in your heart. This passage makes it so clear. When we call on God, He will answer us. When we are in trouble, He is with us. He is our defender and protector. The root of our parenting anxiety is found in believing the lie that says, *The world is unsafe. My children aren't safe. I can't do enough to keep them safe no matter how hard I try. They're going to get hurt, so I cannot ever rest.* But these thoughts are based on the lie that God isn't who He says He is.

WHEN WE CHOOSE TO OPERATE FROM A PLACE OF ASSURANCE IN THE POWER OF GOD RATHER THAN FEAR OF THE DANGERS OF THE WORLD, WE CAN REST IN THE PEACE THAT COMES FROM COPARENTING WITH THE ONE WHO CREATED THE UNIVERSE.

God has not stopped shepherding us as we care for our kids. He loves our children even more than we do! And when we choose to operate from a place of assurance in the power of God rather than fear of the dangers of the world, we can rest in the peace that comes from coparenting with the one who created the universe—the one who gave us children so that through us they could find their way back to Him. They've always been His. And He has always been enough for all of us.

LET'S PRAY TOGETHER

Father, while we are awakened to the terrible reality of evil, we know we don't walk through this world or guide our children through this world unguarded. Your Word says You are our defender. You are our protector. You are our shield.

When fear or anxiety tries to remind us just how dangerous the world is for us or for our children, help us drag those tormenting distractions to the cross, where we can point and say, "That is where Jesus overcame everything I would ever face. That is where He pledged to help me. That is where He promised to love and protect not just me but also my kids."

Lord, help us anchor our hearts in truth this week to uproot every lie and anxiety. Help us come to You quickly to process information and make our decisions in light of the completed work of Jesus. And help us recognize when we need to ask for help from those around us. Send Your Spirit to fill our hearts with peace now. We ask in Jesus's name. Amen.

Say This with Me

God is involved in each of my days, and He loves my children more than I do. He will help me. He will lead me. He will give me wisdom. He will fill my heart with peace as I trust Him.

Try This

Write out Psalm 91 and include your children's names in this prayer. Place this note where you can see it daily to remind yourself that God is protecting your children.

4

Holy Spirit Wilderness Guide

WE DON'T HAVE TO BE AFRAID BECAUSE WE ARE NEVER ALONE

A few years ago as I was recovering from major surgery, my husband and I found a new television show. We are the kind of couple who like to watch all the available episodes of one show before we start another. I guess they call it bingeing, and that summer, that's exactly what we did. I couldn't get around very well, but fortunately, my momma and my husband's momma helped out so much with our kids during that time! But I did need something to keep me entertained for the hours I had to sit and recover.

Just a few days into recovery, before my momma took the kids to play so I could rest awhile, she asked if we had heard of the show *Alone*. Intrigued, we asked her to tell us more about it. The basic premise is this: Ten contestants are dropped off in the wilderness with a limited amount of survival gear. They are given their own areas to make their homes, and they are completely isolated from one other and the rest of the world. With the exception of random medical check-ins, no one is around, not even film crews. Participants must self-document their entire experiences, setting up camera equipment and recording their personal journeys.

The person who lasts the longest out in the wilderness wins a half-million dollars. Contestants can tap out anytime and use the radios they are given to call for a rescue. If they fail a medical check-in, they can also be sent home and forced to leave the game. Because the contestants are isolated, the final one has no idea he is the last one standing until a loved one shows up during a fake medical check-in and tells him he has survived alone the longest.

Since first hearing about this show, my husband and I have watched many of the seasons available on streaming services. I mean, we've virtually become experts at surviving in the wild at this point. We know how to start a fire if something happens to our ferro rod (a fire-starting tool many contestants choose to bring as one of their items). We know how to create a basic lean-to shelter and how different mossy grasses can be used to block wind in a more complex shelter. We know how to set a gill net in the water for salmon. We know how to rig a Paiute deadfall to catch small critters and how to avoid getting sick from eating a muskrat. We know what scat is, how to spot fresh scat, and why fresh scat might be one of the most dangerous things to find in the forest. We have also learned how much survivalists love to say the word *scat* on camera. We could totally go into the wilderness and survive if we had to, except we actually couldn't at all. You know what I mean?

The point is, we've learned and seen so much watching all these episodes that we really feel as though we've seen it all. We know what to expect, and we aren't really shocked by much now that we are "experts." We've seen contestants go home because of injuries, malnutrition, and fear of predators. We've seen some people tap out on the first day and some just days before winning. We've seen nature send contestants home because even though they are highly trained survivalists, they just couldn't forage enough food or get the fish to bite.

But during a particular season, one contestant completely shocked us. The guy seemed to catch all the breaks. Unlike the other contestants, who were struggling to maintain their caloric intake and fortify their shelters from the wind and rain, he was surviving easily. He established a camp. He found a consistent food source. And rather than stress about just surviving, he spent his days focused on enjoying his time in the wilderness. He made himself a table and chair. He whittled a chess set. He truly made himself at home in the woods. Based on his circumstances, he could have easily outlasted all the other survivalists. He was by far the most skilled and equipped to make it until the end. But (spoiler alert) he didn't win that season.

As I thought about this man's experience, I recognized something profound that he shared with everyone, not through his words but through his actions. This man felt the true depths of the isolation. While the other contestants spent their time trying to find food or survive the cold or make it to the next day, this man's mind was free to wander, and the impact of the isolation sent him home before nature could. He missed his family, and he hit a point where he was tired of being alone. No amount of money could keep him from those he loved.

WE WERE NOT DESIGNED TO BE ALONE.

Friend, you see what this one simple example proves is true: we were not designed to be alone. Our hearts cannot take continuous isolation because at our core, we were made to be in constant relationship with our Creator and one another. The Lord made this very clear from the beginning of time.

Designed for Connection

My dad likes to remind me that we can learn just about everything we need to know about who God is, what His original design for our lives was, and what He has in His heart for us still today if we look back at the Garden of Eden. You probably remember that when God made Adam and Eve and placed them in this garden, they were perfectly cared for. They had constant relationship with Him. They lacked for nothing. They walked with God in the garden. They talked with God in the garden. Life was so, so good in the garden. This is what He wanted for all of us for all eternity. Yes, *all*. God wanted all of us to grow up in a world like the garden.

Really? Yep! Where does it say that in Scripture, though? Well, most people skip right over the fact that the very first instruction God gave to Adam and Eve was "Be fruitful and increase in number; fill the earth and subdue it. Rule over

the fish in the sea and the birds in the sky and over every living creature that moves on the ground."[1] This was before
God gave instructions about which trees Adam and Eve
could and couldn't eat. This was before Adam and Eve sinned
and separation came between God and humankind. These
were the first words God spoke to humanity. Can you imagine if Adam and Eve had listened to God's instructions and
never sinned?

God never meant for humanity to exist outside His consistent presence in our lives. We were never supposed to
have to think about or plan or deal with the day-to-day
things in life without God's constant guiding. We were all
supposed to have the same relationship with the Lord that
Adam and Eve had. But that obviously didn't happen. When
sin entered the world and separation came between God and
His creation, everything changed.

You know the story from here. With sin and separation
came death. Death in all forms. But God wasn't surprised.
Scripture says in Revelation 13:8 that Jesus was "the Lamb
slain from the foundation of the world" (NKJV). Before humankind even had a chance to sin, God had already prepared
a way for them to return to Him. Jesus came and reconciled
our estranged relationships with the Father through His
sacrifice. Now when we accept Jesus's death as the payment
for our separated status, we have access to God as He originally intended it. We are still walking through a broken
world, but we have the same access to God that Adam and
Eve had in the garden.

Why is this important? Because we were not designed to
exist alone, and deep in the heart of every person is the long-

ing to return to Eden. Can I say something here? I know that you know this. I know that you have heard about the access you have to God. I know that pastors and teachers and blog posts and podcasts remind us all the time that we can go directly to God because we are no longer separated by the wedge of sin. This isn't news, right? You know it. You've been taught it. These are the facts of our salvation and relationship with God. But I think there is a disconnect between what we've been told and what we believe deeply in our hearts. And if the disconnect isn't between what we've been told and what we believe, then it's between what we believe and how we live.

WE ARE FULLY CONNECTED TO GOD, BUT WE WALK AROUND AS IF HE IS AN ETERNITY AWAY.

Let's talk about this for just a second. We know that we have access to God, but would you agree that most Christians you know do not recognize in their day-to-day lives the presence of God invading every situation? (I'm raising my own hand here.) It's like we know it, but it never settles into our hearts to the point that it influences our actions. We are fully connected to God, but we walk around as if He is an eternity away.

Think about it: When you wake up, is the first thing on your mind *I'm a supernatural being, connected to the Creator of the universe?* Probably not. You're probably thinking about feeding your baby, getting your kids ready for school, and starting the day. You're wondering what's ahead. You're worried about taking care of all the things on your to-do list. The world around us is very, very real. But the supernatural world is just as real; we simply struggle to remember that.

Paul, one of the men in the Bible most devoted to God, even said, "I do not understand what I do. For what I want to do I do not do, but what I hate I do."[2] Basically, "I know what I want to do. I know how I want to live. But I don't do it. And all the stuff that I really despise, I do!" He was pointing out that he was bound to the body he lived in, even though he knew he was called to another way of living. Paul went on to say, "Those who live according to the flesh have their minds set on what the flesh desires; but those who live in accordance with the Spirit have their minds set on what the Spirit desires."[3] He was reminding the church members in Rome that they were able to choose how they would live. Through this letter, Paul reminds us today that there is another way to live. What he said after this is very important. I want you to think about Paul writing this letter to you. So put your name in the blanks:

> You, _____, however, are not in the realm of the flesh but are in the realm of the Spirit, if indeed the Spirit of God lives in you. And if anyone does not have the Spirit of Christ, they do not belong to Christ. But if Christ is in you, _____, then even though your body is subject to death because of sin, the Spirit gives life because of righteousness. And if the Spirit of him who raised Jesus from the dead is living in you,

_____, he who raised Christ from the dead will also give life to your mortal bod[y] because of his Spirit who lives in you.[4]

We have a hard time remembering that the supernatural is very much a part of the everyday life of the believer, but look at what Paul just reminded us! Christ is in you! The Spirit of Him who raised Jesus from the dead is living in you! Living . . . in . . . you! How? Well, to move forward, we must do a quick recap on who this Spirit really is. I promise, this information—even just reviewing it—is vital to overcoming a common lie that often steals our peace. So review with me.

Who Is the Holy Spirit?

Just before Jesus went to the cross, He told His best friends some really important news, and I'm glad they did their job to go and tell the rest of the world so we would find out this truth today! Jesus said to them, "If you love me, keep my commands. And I will ask the Father, and he will give you *another advocate* to help you and be with you forever—the Spirit of truth. The world cannot accept him, because it neither sees him nor knows him. But you know him, for he lives with you and will be in you."[5]

Jesus was promising the Holy Spirit. This is the Spirit who Paul referred to in the book of Romans. It's important to point out that the Greek words Jesus used for "another

advocate" in the scripture we just read were *allos parakletos.*
Parakletos is translated as "helper or advocate."[6] The word
used for "another," *allos,* can mean "another of the same kind."[7]
Why are you giving me Greek lessons, Becky? I'm telling you
what these words mean because we need to see that Jesus
promised to send another helper just like Himself. Some
translations even say "another Comforter." Looking at this
scripture with the words Jesus used, He said, "I will ask the
Father, and he will give you another helper of the same kind
to help you and be with you forever." The Holy Spirit isn't
some random spirit or some obscure version of God that we
cannot comprehend; He is the Spirit of God.

Let's look at some basic facts. The Holy Spirit is referred
to as "the Lord" in 2 Corinthians 3:17: "The Lord is the Spirit,
and where the Spirit of the Lord is, there is freedom." The
Holy Spirit is a person, not a thing. Jesus Himself called the
Holy Spirit "he" in John 16:13: "When he, the Spirit of truth,
comes, he will guide you into all the truth. He will not speak
on his own; he will speak only what he hears, and he will tell
you what is yet to come." We know that the Holy Spirit has
emotions because Scripture tells us He can be grieved. We
know that He can speak because Jesus said it was true. We
know that He can guide because Scripture tells us it's true.
Do I need to go on?

The Holy Spirit is the Spirit of God, and Paul reminds us
this is powerful, because God's "Spirit searches out everything and shows us God's deep secrets. No one can know a
person's thoughts except that person's own spirit, and no one
can know God's thoughts except God's own Spirit. And we

have received God's Spirit (not the world's spirit), so we can know the wonderful things God has freely given us."[8]

The Spirit of God lives inside you!

This is pretty incredible stuff. I'm going to repeat myself and see if it settles into your heart today a little differently than it did perhaps yesterday: the Spirit of God lives inside you!

These are the same words I told my nearly ten-year-old son last night. We were having a conversation about the Holy Spirit, and as I was explaining, he had an aha moment and said, "You know, I've always just sort of thought of the Holy Spirit as God's friend. I didn't really think of Him as God." I think if we are honest, this is how much of the body of Christ treats the Spirit of God. But Scripture is so clear. The Holy Spirit is God. He is the Spirit of God.

The Holy Spirit was there at creation, hovering over the face of the water. He was there at the conception of Jesus. He led Jesus into the wilderness to be tested. It was through the power of the Holy Spirit that Jesus cast out demons. He raised Jesus from the dead. And Jesus even said in John 16 that it was good for Him to go to His Father in heaven so that He could send us His Holy Spirit. "In fact, it is best for you that I go away, because if I don't, the Advocate won't come. If I do go away, then I will send him to you."[9]

Jesus couldn't have made it any clearer. Often He spoke in parables, but here He spoke plainly. "Yes, I'm going to the

Father, but I'm sending you another comforter just like Me! He will teach you and remind you of what I said. I'm leaving My peace with you! It's good that I'm going so He can come!" Pause and take a quick assessment of how you feel. Is this stirring something inside you? Is your heart awakening to the reality that the Spirit of God lives inside you even this minute?

Super-Natural Supernatural

Discussing the supernatural can make many of us feel a little uneasy. It's different. It's big. Because many don't understand it, they don't teach about it. We always want to make sure what we believe is true and biblical. So, I hope that even if you haven't had much study on this topic in the past, you see now that the supernatural is the foundation of Christian life. After all, you already believe in supernatural things.

You believe that Jesus, the Son of God, came and walked the earth. He was born, just as you and I were born. He grew up here. He lived to about the same age I am right now before His journey led Him to the cross. Then He died. He gave up His spirit, and through His ultimate sacrifice as fully God and fully man, He broke the curse of sin and death for all who would accept His sacrifice. Then He came back and walked the earth a little more, but this time He did some cool appearing and disappearing. He walked through locked doors, and then He floated up through the clouds into heaven. Those facts are so common that we forget just how supernatural they are.

But you believe all that, right? You believe that really happened? You believe that at some point, you will take your last breath in this body that will remain on earth without your spirit and that your spirit will supernaturally come alive in another body in heaven, right? You believe that Jesus's supernatural death and resurrection made a way for that to happen? Because your salvation is contingent on those facts being true. Across all denominations, this is the core of the Christian faith. This is what the Bible says is true. So this is what we believe.

The reason I ask is because if you can believe all that, then you know that the supernatural is just as real as the natural world around you this minute. Pause. Look up. Take in everything you see with your eyes. And remember that the unseen world around you is just as real as the laundry pile in your house, the jarred food at the back of your refrigerator, the toilet paper in your bathroom, and the pillow on your bed. It's real, sis. *Real.*

You're real. I'm real. The Holy Spirit is real. Let's take this talk full circle and chat for a minute about God's presence with us. I said you have the same access to God as Adam and Eve did, and they walked with Him. So, how is this true for us? How did Jesus make a way for us to have access to God in the same way they did in the garden? We cannot see Him in a body. We cannot always talk with Him audibly. But we have been given the Spirit of the Lord to live within us and guide us every day.

Imagine you are in the room you're in right now. It shouldn't be hard. You're there, after all. Imagine the day was just as it has been leading up to this point. Imagine you are reading this book. Now imagine I prompt you to look up suddenly. If you're on an airplane or in a vehicle or sitting in a doctor's office, just follow me here. You look up from the book you hold in your hands, and Jesus walks in, smiling, happy, so proud of you. Jesus the friend. Jesus the fisherman. Jesus the carpenter and the man's man. Jesus . . . maybe with a man bun? But Jesus, King of kings, Lord of lords, and your best friend. Your biggest fan. Your biggest cheerleader. The one who counts all your victories and who sinks all your failures into a sea of forgetfulness. *Jesus!*

He rushes over to you, and immediately this deep peace settles around you. His presence isn't just as a man but as a spirit who changes the atmosphere around you and within you. You can tangibly sense His presence changing every part of your environment, and you are overwhelmed. You worship. You hug Him. You fall at His feet, and He laughs, sharing His joy with you like a gift and good medicine.

You know you will never be the same. You know your life from this moment on will be marked by this encounter that changed everything you believe to be true and real. You know you cannot move forward from this moment the same as you were, and you know you will never settle for anything less than His presence in your life every day. You are in all ways undone and remade.

Okay, now I want you to remember that Jesus is currently seated at the right hand of the Father. He said He'd come again to judge the living and the dead. He said He'd return, and He also said He wouldn't leave us as orphans but would give us His Holy Spirit.

What if we viewed the Holy Spirit with the same awe and wonder as we do Jesus? When we pray and ask God to come close and help us, He sends His Spirit. When we say, *Lord, I need You! Show me what to do,* it's the Holy Spirit who gives us wisdom. Scripture reminds us that the Holy Spirit came upon Jesus. Scripture reminds us that the Spirit led Him. Scripture reminds us that Jesus cast out demons by the Spirit. The Holy Spirit was instrumental in the birth, ministry, and resurrection of Jesus. We've already discussed this. He's not weird. He's not foreign. He is God.

So, sweet sister of mine, that same Spirit—the one who feels like Jesus, the one who filled Jesus, the one who caused Jesus to say it was good for Him to leave so He could send you this Spirit—is with you this minute.

Put your hand on your chest. *That close.*

Breathe in and out. *That close.*

Interacting with Him is simple . . . truly. Much simpler than it seems. And it starts by simply acknowledging His presence. So, let's quickly pause for prayer.

Father, thank You for sending Your Spirit. Thank You for not leaving me alone but sending a comforter. Thank You for being with me, even when I don't see You physically in the room. Fill my heart now with Your love. Help me feel how close You really are in this moment. No matter what's going on around me, You are here. Awaken my heart to this truth. I ask in Jesus's name. Amen.

Never Alone

....

How does this conversation about the Holy Spirit have anything to do with the anxiety we face? Sis, one of the most ridiculous lies the Enemy tries to use to keep us discouraged is the idea that we are all alone. Talk about crazy. The Enemy is the one who is crazy. The Enemy comes in with his whispered lies and says junk like, "No one gets it. No one sees you. No one knows how you feel or how hard it is to be you. Your suffering isn't noticed. You've got to figure it out and carry it on your own." It's so gross, but we must admit that those thoughts or similar ones have slipped into our minds in the past.

> # You are, in fact, never alone. Ever. The Spirit of God never leaves you.

But these lies couldn't be further from the truth. You are, in fact, never alone. Ever. The Spirit of God never leaves you. The psalmist put it like this in 139:7–10:

> Where can I go from your Spirit?
>   Where can I flee from your presence?
> If I go up to the heavens, you are there;
>   if I make my bed in the depths, you are there.
> If I rise on the wings of the dawn,

if I settle on the far side of the sea,
even there your hand will guide me,
your right hand will hold me fast.

Yet we so often forget. We act as though we must find our own way. We act as though we must get ourselves out of every dark place. We act as though the Holy Spirit pops in and out of our lives to give us advice and then leaves. Why? Because we become distracted by what we see, what we feel, and what we think rather than what we *know* deep within us. We forget that we've been given the Spirit of God to guide us through every situation and storm.

There is no place where we can hide from God's presence in our lives. Yet we can very easily ignore Him. We can become so focused on the wind and waves around us that we forget Jesus is standing right there with us. And we forget Jesus is Peace Himself.

So, I'm going to propose something here. Your body can misfire chemicals and have incorrect balances that make your heart race, but you still have peace within you. You can be walking through seasons of sadness or struggle and still have peace within you. You can be doing well and have peace within you. You can be hurting and have peace within you. Because Jesus is peace and His peace doesn't leave you.

Friend, something powerful happens when we remember that what we feel in our bodies and what we experience around us aren't all there is. Something amazingly powerful happens inside us when we realize that the supernatural is just as real as what we are experiencing in the natural and when we invite the Lord to help us shift our hearts from what we see and feel to what is true. Our hearts become empowered by the Spirit of God inside us, who overwhelms every fear with His love.

I don't know what your life looks like right now. I don't know how your heart feels, how your body feels, how your mind feels. I don't know what your circumstances look like. I don't know if things are great or if you're teetering on the edge of what seems like a bottomless pit. But I know that if you ask God to give you His supernatural peace in the middle of this moment, He will. Not because you said the right words. Not because you prayed the right way. Not because you earned it or deserved it. But because Jesus made a way for you to never be alone. And when God's presence rises up inside you, it pushes back the darkness. Friend, you are never alone. Never alone. Never alone.

When no one is around . . . Never alone.

When it feels as though no one cares . . . Never alone.

When it seems as if it's all on you . . . Never alone.

When the Enemy wants to tell you differently . . . You are, in fact, never alone.

Let's Pray Together

Father, thank You for the gift of Your constant presence. No matter what is happening in our lives, remind us again and again that You haven't left us. In this world, we will have trouble. Your Word even says this is true. The gift of a Christian life isn't a life free from difficulties. The gift of a Christian life is the ever-present relationship we have with You, no matter what we are walking through day to day.

Lord, on the days when anxiety wants to be all that we see and feel, help us perceive the supernatural world around us and within us. Help us remember that You give us Your peace. Help us cry out for Your Spirit to overcome every fear that might try to steal from our lives. Help us stay awake to Your presence constantly. We ask in Jesus's name. Amen.

Say This with Me
. . . .

The Holy Spirit never leaves me. I have power because He is with me. I have peace within me always because He is with me always. I am never alone.

Try This
. . . .

Take a moment to welcome the Holy Spirit, acknowledging God's presence right where you are. Thank Him for giving you His Peace. Ask Him to remind you of His presence throughout the coming days.

5

Trail Angels

We Need One Another to Overcome Anxiety

I had vaguely heard of the Pacific Crest Trail before moving to Southern California. I saw a few minutes of a movie, or maybe just the trailer, about the true story of a young woman who decided to hike part of the massive path that runs from the border of Mexico to the border of Canada to rediscover herself after some tragic personal events. It was an intriguing story, but it wasn't one I could relate to in any way, the first reason being I do not hike.

This might not come as a surprise. If you've read my other books, you know I don't run unless something is chasing me. I personally believe Proverbs 28:1 should be taken more seriously. It says, "The wicked run away when no one is chasing them."[1]

I hope my sarcasm is coming through here. Truthfully, that scripture is more of an allegory on bravery and standing your ground, but I digress. The point is, I don't run because I don't enjoy it, and hiking is right there on the same shelf

I'm not grabbing from when it comes to things I'd choose to do for fun.

Wanna run? Nope. No, thank you. *Wanna put on a back-pack and hike? On purpose?* Not today. I'll pass. *Come on! Don't you want to test your own limits? Stretch yourself? Take on new heights and get a different perspective on life?* That's about the last thing I feel like doing ever, thank you. Remember, I was born and raised in Oklahoma. Where I come from it's so flat you can see just about as far as the natural curvature of the earth if a cow or a tree isn't in your way.

It's F-L-A-T.

Hiking is not part of who I am or how I was raised, and it's just not how I choose to enjoy the world. Let's be honest: I strongly disliked the fact that at the school my kids attended in Southern California, parents were required to park and then walk up a hill to drop off their kids. Up the hill to drop them off, back down to the car. Up the hill to pick them up, back down to the car. Up the hill and back down for each of my three kids' separate drop-off and pick-up times—three separate round trips each day. Definitely wasn't my favorite thing in the world, but I felt like it almost qualified me as a hiker! If you ask me to hike with you, my answer is kindly going to be "No, thanks."

However, that doesn't mean hiking isn't interesting to me. I actually find it fascinating. The idea of stripping away everything except what's essential for survival, planning and prepping, gathering gear, and placing that pack on my back and heading off into the wilderness to get away from the world is a pretty attractive concept (especially for a mom who drives a van that's usually full of both people and unnecessary junk every day). But the most intriguing thing I've learned about the hiking community is that entire groups of people spend their free time helping hikers.

What do I mean? While there are brave and wild adventurers who take on extensive expeditions such as the Pacific Crest Trail, hiking the entire 2,600-plus miles from Mexico to Canada, there are also organizations dedicated to simply helping these hikers along the way. These helpers who perform random acts of hiking kindness are often referred to as trail angels.

Some trail angels wait on the path with fresh water. Others volunteer to drive hikers from the trail into nearby towns so they can refill their rations before the next phase of their journey. Some take hikers into their homes for the night and drive them back to the trail refreshed the next morning. Others cook and bring food to the path so hikers can refuel their energy with a warm meal in their bellies. It's all so very remarkable!

But my personal favorites are the trail angels who set out on the trail without a pack of their own, hoping to find hikers who will allow them to carry their packs a few miles. Let's imagine this scenario for just a second. Many of these hikers have prepared to spend months carrying on their backs everything they need to survive. They have hiked many miles every single day with that load they can't afford to leave behind, and then as they hit, let's say, mile number 800 of 2,600, Tracy Trail Angel shows up and says, "Can I carry that for you? I know you must be so tired, and you have a long way to go."

Can you imagine the pure relief? I mean, I cannot personally understand what it would feel like to pass that heavy pack to a stranger and say, "Okay. Thank you. You may carry the full weight of my burden." Don't get me wrong. I've carried a sleeping second grader in from the car and up to her bed. I know the success of making it up the stairs with the kid still asleep and the relief of laying her down without waking her up. But carrying the equivalent amount of weight for months? All day? Knowing it's never going to get any lighter? And then having someone say "Let me take that for you"? I don't think I can imagine that kind of liberation.

But maybe I can. Maybe being a trail angel and carrying someone's pack for a few miles isn't a concept found only in the world of hikers. Maybe this is exactly what God had in mind when He told us to "carry each other's burdens, and in this way you will fulfill the law of Christ."[2] Maybe He envisioned us purposefully stepping into the lives of others and offering a listening ear to give them a place to share their cares and fears. Maybe He saw us walking with others who need the hope we carry in our hearts or the strategy for freedom found in our stories.

Maybe we should all be prepared to be trail angels whenever the opportunities arise. Because we are all carrying much more than most people realize, and we never know when the Lord is going to ask us to help our friends or even perfect strangers walk through fear or frustration. Strangers like the woman I met one midweek afternoon.

A Pack Full of Grief

·····································

It was a regular Wednesday when the Lord sent me to the store to run an errand. I thought I was simply going to pick something up from a nearby business, but the Lord was actually sending me to the store on assignment.

I stood looking at a wall of products, trying to decide which I needed, when I noticed another mom about my age shopping as well. I made a joke about how there were just too many options and wondered out loud how I was ever supposed to decide which one was right. She didn't look at me. She seemed quiet, but most moms in Los Angeles seem so in comparison to my midwestern "everyone is my best friend; never met a gal I didn't like" approach to strangers.

In fairness, she was just shopping and deep in thought. She didn't seem unusually silent. Well, she didn't seem so at first. We ended up making small talk about being moms, and we both brought up our children. It seemed like any other encounter with a mom on a random Wednesday . . . until she paused and then told me her daughter had passed away very unexpectedly just a few weeks before.

I looked over at her and instantly saw what the Lord had sent me to do. I was supposed to help carry her pack for a while. In the middle of that store on a regular weekday, with Michael Jackson's "Man in the Mirror" playing over the speakers, I whispered, "I'm so sorry. Will you tell me about your daughter?" Her eyes filled with tears, and she shared her whole story. This precious momma told me the circumstances surrounding her daughter's passing, how her family was coping, and how she really felt: guilty, ashamed, angry, broken, unsure of herself, vulnerable, and lost.

For the next hour and a half, I listened. I didn't just listen to her story; I listened to her heart. I listened for the places where fear was telling her it was her fault. I listened for the little phrases that told me she was believing lies about who she was as a daughter of God and a mom. And as I listened, I spoke truth over every place she needed fresh hope. "It wasn't your fault." "You're such a good momma." "The Lord doesn't want you to believe that this happened because you didn't pray harder."

I shared some of my own story of loss and heartache. I told her about places where I questioned God's goodness. And then I told her that God was big enough to carry her and her grief. I told her He could take all her questions without becoming angry with her. I reminded her that He wept over the loss of his friend Lazarus, and I believe He weeps over each loss here on earth. God is still brokenhearted by the brokenness that originated with sin. As I told her truth, I knew it was hard for her to believe it. I knew it was hard for her heart to receive it fully. Pain can do that.

But most importantly, that afternoon we walked together. We walked right into her grief as strangers and came out together a few miles down the road. We didn't take any physical ground. As a matter of fact, we didn't move from that aisle for nearly two hours. But for that short while, I helped her carry the weight of her sorrow and created a safe place for her to share her pain without any judgment or expectations.

At times we paused to cry together. And none of it felt

strange or out of place. It didn't seem as though it should be reserved for a counselor's office or pastoral meeting. It didn't seem as if we shouldn't be doing what we were doing in a public place on a Wednesday. It felt as natural as reaching up and choosing the can of corn off the shelf and taking it home to make soup. It felt as if there was no other place I needed to be or nothing else I was supposed to be doing other than stopping my day to carry the full weight of her burden for a few hours so she didn't have to process her sorrow alone.

This is why it is so important to obediently do exactly what God asks us to do, go where He asks us to go, and say what He asks us to say, even in the middle of our own agendas. We don't always go to the store expecting to be trail angels, and we don't often leave our own packs at home with the intention of finding someone else's to carry. But we should never overlook the very real opportunities around us to say to friends, family, and even strangers, "Can I walk with you for a while? Can I help you carry your burden?" We desperately need one another, whether we want to admit it or not.

The truth is, we are all both of the women who stood in the store that day. We may not be going through deep grief, or maybe we are. We might not have faced recent tragedy, or perhaps we have. But we are all just travelers passing through this world on our way to the next, and we should eagerly look to carry others' burdens and share ours along the way.

GOD HAS GIVEN US THE GIFT OF ONE ANOTHER, AND THIS GIFT MIGHT JUST HOLD A KEY THAT UNLOCKS ANOTHER LAYER OF HOPE AND HEALING.

God has given us the gift of His presence. We know we don't walk any road alone because the Holy Spirit is always with us. But sometimes we forget that the Lord has given us another gift in addition to His love. God has given us the gift of one another, and this gift might just hold a key that unlocks another layer of hope and healing.

We Were Never Supposed to Walk Alone

Tell me if this sounds familiar: You are in charge of it all. You handle the doctors' appointments, school sign-ups, toddler meltdowns, middle-of-the-night bad dreams, sheet changes, rash assessments, food-allergy supervision, babyproofing, teenager supervision, middle-school managing, sports-practice shuttling, and overall family-calendar keeping around the clock. You manage everyone's hopes, dreams, plans, and problems. You know what's in your refrigerator (or what's not) and when you need to replace the toilet paper and laundry soap. You keep track of all of it.

And it doesn't matter if you've been a mom for one year or eighteen years or thirty years. You're exhausted because running this whole show takes work. It takes all of you. Keeping up with the running lists and schedules in your mind, the constant worries and fears, the never-ending to-do list, and the constant shepherding of your children's hearts toward hope and happiness is around-the-clock work.

Yet despite all we do, it never seems to be enough. We look around and feel as if there is always so much more to be done and we are never going to catch up or be able to do it all. We believe we are never going to get to the bottom of the laundry pile or the bills or check off all the daily duties that are draining the life from us. We look ahead and cannot see a place where the stresses seem to thin. We cannot see a place where expectations will slow and we will catch up on the obligations that seem to overshadow us. We are desperate for help and in need of grace, and instead of thinking *Wow! I do so much! I'm amazing!* we silently shame ourselves for not being able to do it all and for not being happier while we struggle. Rather than celebrate our achievements, we fault ourselves for our feelings: *If I was just able to catch up, my family would be happier. My kids would have a momma who isn't frustrated or short or fussy. If my kids had a more organized or less anxious or less overwhelmed momma, they'd be happier. It's all my fault. I'm trying my hardest, but I can't do it all. And if I just could, everything would be better.*

Momma, don't you see what we do? We pile up our family's hopes and expectations and needs, place them on our own shoulders, and then tell ourselves we cannot ever stop to rest. We tell ourselves that it really is up to us to keep everyone happy. We believe that any issue we cannot correct in our families is a result of our failure as women. If you're honest, is that true? Do you ever think that way or treat yourself that way?

I'm not asking if it's true that you're responsible for your family's happiness or suggesting you are responsible for figuring everything out. I'm asking you to consider whether you feel as though you're carrying the full weight of your family's hope on your shoulders.

Sis! I've said it before, and I'll say it again. No wonder we are anxious. We never get a break from what we have to do, and we never get a break from our own expectations either. But God did not intend for us to do any of this on our own. We were always meant to live in constant relationship with Him *and* with one another.

Community Garden

Let's take a quick trip back to the Garden of Eden. God said it wasn't good for man to be alone, so He created Eve. God knew that Adam had access to Him. God knew that He wasn't going to leave Adam alone. But Adam didn't have a helper like himself whom he could fellowship with and walk alongside and who would understand what it was like to be fully human. So God made woman. And then Adam and Eve had each other. They were able to walk together, take care of the garden and animals together, explore together, eat fruit (even the wrong kind—oops!) together. Most important, they were able to live life alongside each other. God knew this was key to their health and happiness.

The same principle is important in our lives today. If God said it wasn't good for Adam to be alone—back before sin entered the world and everything was perfect and as God intended it to be—how much more do we need one another today on the other side of the garden? God still wants us to do life with one another. He still wants us to pull from the strengths of others. To go to Him when we need help but also to reach out to one another when we feel as if we have exhausted our own hope, faith, patience, and anything else we need. To cry out "I'm sinking over here!" when we feel as though we are drowning and cannot catch a break. But for many of us moms, true connection with one another is hard.

Our schedules, our responsibilities, our coming and going, and everything that's involved with being a mom can make deep friendship feel impossible. Does that ever feel true for you? Most of us know we need community, but we just don't know how to make it happen. As a result, when I talk with moms across the country, one subject comes up again and again—loneliness.

But what most moms don't know is that science has proven a clear link between loneliness and anxiety. I recently read an article that discussed the effects of loneliness on mental health. This article explained that when people feel disconnected from others, their bodies experience "a constant state of mild stress." The article went on to say, "The brain is our main social organ, and feeling lonely may affect regions of the brain that help regulate emotion or manage stress and anxiety."[3] It's an interesting thought, isn't it? The idea that our health could improve by finding time to truly connect with other moms who get us? I just love when science proves what God has already said is true: "It is not good that man should be alone."[4]

Do you want to know something else that's remarkable? In 2018, the UK appointed a "minister for loneliness."[5] The government saw a clear link between loneliness and illness, and an official position was created to help address the condition. I point this out because it drives home the fact that loneliness is not a simple problem we can afford to ignore. We don't just need one another because we can't do it all on our own. We need one another because our health depends on it.

So, what does connection look like in this season of your life? It might look different for you than it does for me. It's going to look different for you in this season than it did in previous seasons or than it will in future seasons. If you have a newborn, it might look like having someone sit with you or fold your clothes or just come over and hold the baby so you can breathe and tell that person how you feel. If you have toddlers, it might look like having an unscheduled playdate in a messy house, where you and another mom talk about how you're both really doing. If you have older kids, it might look like saying to a friend, "My house isn't put together. My life isn't put together. Can you just come and hang with me and be a human who isn't asking me for anything?" It might look like asking that mom friend from church, "Can you meet me for coffee and listen while I tell you about my anxiety or depression or defiant kids or marriage that is in a hard season?"

Pause for just a second to think about how you can connect with a friend this week, whether in person, over the phone, or through Skype or FaceTime. It might not be perfect. It might not be easy. But we all need connection more than we realize. We all need friends who will carry our burdens and place them at Jesus's feet.

Friends Who Will Carry You

A few men in Scripture knew exactly what it means to carry a friend to the feet of Jesus. After all, they physically carried their friend and placed him at Jesus's feet. You probably know this story, found in Luke 5. It's short. Scripture describes it like this:

> One day while Jesus was teaching, some Pharisees and teachers of religious law were sitting nearby. (It seemed that these men showed up from every village in all Galilee and Judea, as well as from Jerusalem.) And the Lord's healing power was strongly with Jesus.
>
> Some men came carrying a paralyzed man on a sleeping mat. They tried to take him inside to Jesus, but they couldn't reach him because of the crowd. So they went up to the roof and took off some tiles. Then they lowered the sick man on his mat down into the crowd, right in front of Jesus. Seeing their faith, Jesus said to the man, "Young man, your sins are forgiven."
>
> But the Pharisees and teachers of religious law said

to themselves, "Who does he think he is? That's blasphemy! Only God can forgive sins!"

Jesus knew what they were thinking, so he asked them, "Why do you question this in your hearts? Is it easier to say 'Your sins are forgiven,' or 'Stand up and walk'? So I will prove to you that the Son of Man has the authority on earth to forgive sins." Then Jesus turned to the paralyzed man and said, "Stand up, pick up your mat, and go home!"

And immediately, as everyone watched, the man jumped up, picked up his mat, and went home praising God. Everyone was gripped with great wonder and awe, and they praised God, exclaiming, "We have seen amazing things today!"[6]

So much happened in this short passage. Jesus taught some religious folks a lesson. He revealed God's healing power. He demonstrated His ability to forgive sins. But at the center of this narrative is a story about friends who would do anything to help their buddy in need. I wish I could have been there for the pre-event meeting these guys had before trying to get their friend to Jesus.

I wonder how many men there were. Scripture doesn't say how many were involved in total. Mark 2:3 says, "Some men came, bringing to him [Jesus] a paralyzed man, carried by four of them." Were there just the four? Were there ten? How many guys were in on this? All we know is that there were at least four guys. So, let's picture just them, for the sake of our story. Can you imagine what they might have said?

Friend One: "Have you heard of this man, Jesus?"

Friend Two: "He's the Nazarene who has been healing everyone brought to him."

Friend Three: "Everyone?!"

Friend Four: "Yes! Everyone! I heard He healed that guy with terrible leprosy."

Man Needing Healing: "Do we know where He is going to be?"

Friend One: "I heard He was passing through town, and I've got this idea."

So, they placed their buddy onto some kind of stretcher and started walking through the streets. It probably wasn't hard to find where Jesus was because of the crowd. Everyone wanted to be near Him. The men tried excusing their way through. They tried pushing their way through. But it must have looked impossible. All Scripture makes clear is that they tried and couldn't get to Jesus.

What did these guys do next? Well, one of them had the idea to use the roof. *If we can't get to Jesus through the door, we'll have to go through the roof,* he must have thought. And so up they went.

Can you picture these guys carrying the full weight of their friend and his mat up to the roof? Taking the stone stairs, climbing over railings, awkwardly lifting their friend, trying their best not to drop him—all motivated by love?

I want friends like that. I want friends who won't just carry me to Jesus in my time of need but who will be willing to find a way to get me to Him no matter the cost. I want friends who will pull tiles from the roof, who will use their full strength to carry and then lower me right to the feet of

Jesus. I want friends of whom Jesus will say, "Because of your faith, she is going to receive her healing."

Did you catch that in the passage? Jesus healed the paralyzed man and set him free not because of his own faith but because of the faith of this man's friends. We need a community who can carry us when our faith is weak. We need friends who will bring us to the Lord in prayer when we feel we cannot bring ourselves. We need friends who will tear open heaven and demand an audience with the King because of their fierce faith, just as these men broke open a roof and brazenly lowered their friend.

Everything changes at the feet of Jesus. You and I both know this is true. Anxiety quiets. Healing comes. Wholeness is possible. Peace is restored. Hope rises. Strength is renewed. Jesus changes everything because He is everything we need. And no matter the state of our physical bodies, our spirits come alive when we come to Him.

WE WERE NEVER MEANT TO DO IT ALL, AND WE WERE NEVER MEANT TO DO IT ALONE. LIFE IS ALWAYS BETTER WHEN WE LIVE IT TOGETHER.

So, let's stop right here and remind Him that we trust Him. Let's tell Him we know He is good and we love Him. But let's also tell Him we need His help. Because something powerful happens when we tell Him what we need. When we pause for a moment and invite the Lord to come close, we acknowledge that we know we were made to need Him. We were designed to need the help of the one who created us, and we were designed to be in community with one another. We were never meant to do it all, and we were never meant to do it alone. Life is always better when we live it together.

LET'S PRAY TOGETHER

Father, Your Word says to come to You and cast our cares on You because You care for us.[7] This week help us continually live out this commission. Help us come to You quickly when we start to feel overwhelmed. Help us come to You quickly when we start to lose our patience. Help us come to You quickly when we need spiritual support and when we need You to send physical support. We don't want to be anxious because we're trying to do what we were never designed to do.

We want to be free from the weight of our own expectations. We can ask for help without shame. We can invite others into our process without feeling like failures. We were created for community, and this week we are going to seek out sisters in the faith who will support us on our journeys toward the peace available at Your feet. You say that we are to bear one another's burdens in love. So we will.

Even though we need help of our own, show

us how to help those around us, Lord. Thank You for lifting the weight of anxiety even now. Thank You for continuing to heal us. Thank You for leading us to the right people, places, and processes that will bring us wholeness. Thank You for loving us and not leaving us in our suffering but lifting us and our hope. We love You, Lord. We ask in Jesus's name. Amen.

Say This with Me

....

It's not up to me to do it all. I will seek out God's help and the help of my community when I need it. I will let Him and those I trust carry my burdens because I'm living out His Word when I do.

Try This

....

Think of one trusted and godly friend you can reach out to and share your heart with this week. Make a plan to connect with this person. Finding someone to walk with you toward hope can be an important part of the healing journey.

6

Fire in the Forest

RECAPTURING THE POWER OF OUR IMAGINATIONS

The day we moved into our new house in Los Angeles, the Santa Ana winds blew violently. These winds are caused by strong air masses from high pressure in the Great Basin area that flow toward the lower pressure coming off the coast. These different pressure systems meet and create swirling winds basically right over my house. I welcomed the wind. It felt like home, really. Oklahoma is known for the wind sweeping down the plains, often bringing a tornado or two with it. At least we wouldn't face any tornadoes here, but these fierce winds would bring another threat.

Not even twenty-four hours after we pulled into our driveway, our neighborhood was put on standby for evacuation, threatened by a wildfire burning just a few miles from our new home. We could see the thick smoke cloud from our front yard, but we didn't know our new area well enough to have an escape route mapped. Which way should we go? What should we bring? What should we plan to take with us? Our belongings were still in boxes, and I wasn't sure I could even find those super valuable treasures you'd want to rescue in an emergency like this.

A neighbor knocked on our door and said we should gather the important stuff and just stay aware. All I could think was *Aware of what? Where am I supposed to get my information so I can stay aware?* In Oklahoma, we have meteorologists who keep us updated about every potential storm. Using radar, they track tornadoes down to the exact mile so people can prepare to take cover if necessary. Where were all the people telling me what to do next?

We turned on the television, but nothing was breaking into the regular programming. Did I need an app? A radio scanner? I will be honest . . . I panicked. Surprise.

Both Jared's and my parents were still in town with us after helping us make the cross-country move, and they were all trying to bring reason to the situation while I was losing my cool. I remember tearing open boxes, desperately looking for photo albums of my babies and my kids' first little onesies that I could put in the back of our van if we needed to leave quickly. Yes, I know they are just things. If the threat had been great, we would have readily left it all behind to save our lives. What heightened my anxiety was the anticipation. We hadn't been told to leave yet. As a matter of fact, locals told us it was all going to be okay and this was normal this time of year.

But it wasn't normal for me. I hadn't lived through anything like this before, and I found myself carrying loads of all the sentimental items I could find to the van. As I made frantic trip after frantic trip, looking to the right and seeing the smoke plume grow darker and closer, I wondered whether

God had really led us across the country to face this wildfire as soon as we arrived.

Let me tell you, we had a conversation about it. *Didn't You tell us to come here, Lord? Didn't You lead each step? Didn't You say to trust Your timing?* My actions didn't indicate trust that the fires wouldn't come. My loading of the back of my van didn't testify to my unyielding faith that God wasn't going to ask us to flee to safer ground. With each box I carried, I said, *I'm afraid. I'm going to prepare for the worst because my imagination is creating an entire scenario where that fire comes sweeping down my street.*

This wasn't the first time a fear of fire had caused me to panic. As I imagined the flames coming toward my new home, I was suddenly back in my childhood bedroom, reliving a fear from the past.

In my memory, it was late at night—well, late for a first grader. It could have been seven thirty for all I know. What I do know for certain is that it was dark outside. The overhead lights in the house had been turned off, the lamps had been turned on in the living room, and from my bedroom, I could hear the low sounds of the television coming down the hall.

Every few minutes, I would peek my head up from my rainbow heart pillow just to make sure the house hadn't gone dark and my parents hadn't gone to bed. I hated to be the last one awake. My thoughts always seemed to race more when I knew that my parents had gone to their bedroom for the night. But falling asleep was so difficult when my mind just couldn't settle . . . and it rarely ever settled.

I stared up at the popcorn ceiling over my bed.

Flames. Thick black smoke and choking flames flashed

across my mind. The house was consumed with fire, and I was trapped in my bedroom alone. The doorway was blocked. I began to picture a scenario that had never taken place in my home, creating a strategy, living each imagined moment as though it were real, thinking through each step.

How would I get out of the house? I'd go to the window and try to open it. But I tried to open it last week, and I couldn't. The chair. I'd have to smash it with the chair. But the glass would get into my eyes. I'd turn my head and hit the window with the wooden chair, and maybe it would break. But I don't know how to get the screen off. The glass would break, but the screen would be stuck. I'd have to crawl out the front door through the fire. But what about Mommy and Daddy? They'd come looking for me. They wouldn't know I got out on my own. They'd be stuck inside, and I'd be safe outside at the Lewises' house next door. I have to tell them. They need to know not to come for me. They won't make it. They'll die in the fire, and it will be all my fault.

I sat up in bed.

"Moooommma! Dadddy!"

I heard the television go silent and footsteps come down the carpeted hall.

"Becky? What is it?"

"Don't come for me if there's a fire. I can get out myself."

"What are you talking about? Of course we will come for you if there's a fire."

"NO! Don't!"

I closed my eyes and could see my parents trapped in my small bedroom, searching for me, wondering where I was. I could see myself outside. Safe. My parents hugged me closely as deep sobs came up from the imagined guilt. Hot tears stung my face. The guilt felt real. The guilt of knowing they had died because of me.

It had never taken place. It would likely never take place. But I had lived it out in my heart as though it did. I had seen each terrifying moment. And I was afraid. The same was true in Los Angeles twenty-five years later. I was imagining a future full of danger, and I was responding as though it were going to happen.

Imagination is powerful like that. Whether we are seven or thirty-two, our imaginations can create entire experiences in our minds that have never happened and likely never will. Yet we live out a physical, mental, and emotional response to imagined events.

Would you agree that your imagination can get the best of you? Maybe you don't fear fire as I did, but maybe you're afraid to take your hand off your toddler in the shopping cart at the store because you've imagined someone snatching her while you have your back turned. Maybe you stay awake at night worrying about your teenager because your imagination has vividly played out a tragic car accident. Maybe you imagine someone breaking into your home or a dangerous situation unfolding at your child's school. And maybe these imagined scenarios keep you from peace because your mind has seen all of them unfold as if they were real.

The thing is, your imagination was not intended to work this way. Our imaginations are gifts God has given to us so we can dream and create with Him, but they have been broken and are now used for both good and evil. Let's go back to the Garden of Eden again. Yes . . . again! Remember, we can learn so much about whom God wanted us to be by looking at what He originally designed.

Here's what Genesis 1:26–27 says:

God said, "Let us make human beings in our image, to be like us. They will reign over the fish in the sea, the birds in the sky, the livestock, all the wild animals on the earth, and the small animals that scurry along the ground."

So God created human beings in his own image.
　In the image of God he created them;
　　male and female he created them.[1]

Did you catch the *us* and *our* in that passage? I love how God the Father, God the Son, and God the Holy Spirit are all represented here. God had this quick conversation with Himself and decided to craft us in His image. He made us like Him. Unlike any of the other creatures, we are made in the image of our creator. Scripture makes this clear, so I want to be clear too.

Genesis 2:7 goes on to describe how this formation happened: "Then the LORD God formed the man from the dust of the ground. He breathed the breath of life into the man's nostrils, and the man became a living person."[2]

God looked into the dirt and didn't see just dirt. He saw a man. He saw a being He had already formed in His heart before He shaped the man from the clay. God had dreams for this creation. He had plans for this man. He breathed life into his body, and the man became alive. This man carried God's attributes. Not just the placement of His eyes and nose or His two arms and strong legs. He carried within him God's character. He held within his heart his own ability to create, just as the Father had created him.

This is important because it is true of all of us. When God made us in His image, He made us dreamers like Him. He gave us the ability to look at something that's *not* and see what *could be*. It's how we design cities and businesses and run countries. It's how we make plans for the future and craft art and roads and technology.

Did you know many scientists agree that our ability to imagine is what sets us apart from the other animals on earth? Without giving credit to God or acknowledging the role He played in our creation, these scientists are proving that we are unlike all the other creatures because we carry the image and capabilities of our creator.

Our imaginations allow us to dream like God, look toward the future with hope like God, design, scheme, and strategize like God. And then we can take steps to create what we design first in our hearts and minds before it ever exists physically around us. What a cool thing that our imaginations are a way in which we glorify the creative and imaginative God who made us!

But something happened at the beginning of time on earth. Our imaginations were hijacked the moment Adam and Eve ate the apple. They had done something the snake suggested rather than what God commanded. And the moment they acted like the snake rather than like God, they were no longer perfect reflections of their creator. God could no longer look at them and see only Himself. He saw the snake's influence. This . . . this is the consequence of sin. Humanity broke and would continue to break forever.

We broke on the cellular level, and our cells now die and mutate. But another important part of who we are also broke as a result of the fall of humanity. Our minds, dreams, and imaginations broke too. Remember, Scripture says that Eve ate from the tree of the knowledge of both good and evil. Up until that point she had known only good, but now her eyes had been opened to both.

Adam and Eve still had the ability to dream and look toward the future, but now they could see both good and evil. They still had the capability of imagining what could be, but they no longer saw the future solely through the filter of love and God's truth. Can you see what happened, friend? Can you see how one of our greatest gifts, the ability to dream with God, was broken by that original sin and handed back to us corrupted?

As for everyone who has lived since Adam and Eve, our eyes have been opened. We know both good and evil. And the very part of us that perhaps makes us the most like God—our capability to imagine and create and look into nothing and pull out only beauty—has been distorted.

Anxiety captures our imaginations and causes us to look toward the future with fear. We imagine realities full of not only love but also danger. You probably know exactly what I'm talking about. You know what it's like to play out all the ways everything can go wrong. You know what it's like to imagine how others might reject you, how someone might leave you, or how you might be embarrassed. You know what it's like to imagine how someone you love could be hurt, how you could be hurt, or how something won't work out and it will be your fault. You know how real fear can feel, and you know all the behaviors that come with feeling anxious and afraid.

Sister, we were made to dream with God, hope with God, plan with God, and look toward the future and trust that He'll be with us. So, how do we take back our creative minds? If we were meant to live in the garden of God's love and light, how do we survive our days in the forest of fear?

We let God remind us that He still sees tomorrow full of promise even when we do not. He still looks toward the future and knows that He will meet us there too.

Jeremiah 29:11 and the Rest of the Story

One of the most well-known and recited verses is Jeremiah 29:11. Can you quote it just from hearing that reference? It says, "'I know the plans I have for you,' declares the LORD, 'plans to prosper you and not to harm you, plans to give you hope and a future.'"

It's no wonder we cling to this verse. God has plans to prosper us. His plans for us are not to harm us. His plans give us hope and a future. He knows His plans, and He leads us toward them. What great comfort these words provide our often-restless hearts! But this verse, frequently plucked from the center of a much longer passage, is actually part of a letter the prophet Jeremiah sent to the exiles living in Babylon.

Exiles? Babylon? What are we talking about here? And why does it matter?

If this verse teaches us that God has good plans for His people, it's important to know the context. So, some background. This letter is found in the book of Jeremiah, which is part of the Old Testament (prior to Jesus walking the earth). Long before Jeremiah lived, God had established His covenant with His people, the Israelites, saying,

> The LORD your God is bringing you into a good land—a land with brooks, streams, and deep springs gushing out into the valleys and hills; a land with wheat and barley, vines and fig trees, pomegranates, olive oil and honey; a land where bread will not be scarce and you will lack nothing; a land where the rocks are iron and you can dig copper out of the hills.
>
> When you have eaten and are satisfied, praise the LORD your God for the good land he has given you.[3]

The Israelites had a promise—a beautiful land of their own—but their obedience was the key that kept them living in the promise God had made for them. God told them what would happen if they stopped obeying His commands:

> Remember the LORD your God. He is the one who gives you power to be successful, in order to fulfill the covenant he confirmed to your ancestors with an oath.
>
> But I assure you of this: If you ever forget the LORD

your God and follow other gods, worshiping and bow-
ing down to them, you will certainly be destroyed. Just
as the LORD has destroyed other nations in your path,
you also will be destroyed if you refuse to obey the
LORD your God.[4]

It seems very clear. God's people were to follow His commands and to be careful not to forget Him. But by the year
587 BC, where the story in Jeremiah picks up, God's people
living in Judah had forgotten their God. They had forgotten
His commands. As a result, they lost the benefits of the
promise.

The kingdom of Judah fell into the hands of the Babylonian king, Nebuchadnezzar. Judah's king, Jehoiachin, sur-
rendered and became Nebuchadnezzar's captive. He wasn't
the only captive. Second Kings 24:14 tells us Nebuchadnezzar "carried all Jerusalem into exile: all the officers and fighting men, and all the skilled workers and artisans—a total of
ten thousand. Only the poorest people of the land were left."

Let me explain what was going on: God's people were living in Babylon. Their kingdom had been exiled. There was
certainly weeping. There was lamenting. As a matter of fact,
it is said that Jeremiah wrote the book of Lamentations
around this time. But it's into this space that God directed
Jeremiah to write His people a letter, and this is what Jeremiah 29 says (emphasis mine):

This is what the LORD Almighty, the God of Israel,
says to all those I carried into exile from Jerusalem to

Babylon: "Build houses and settle down; plant gardens and eat what they produce. Marry and have sons and daughters; find wives for your sons and give your daughters in marriage, so that they too may have sons and daughters. Increase in number there; do not decrease. Also, seek the peace and prosperity of the city to which I have carried you into exile. Pray to the LORD for it, because if it prospers, you too will prosper. . . .

"When seventy years are completed for Babylon, I will come to you and fulfill my good promise to bring you back to this place. *For I know the plans I have for you,*" declares the LORD, *"plans to prosper you and not to harm you, plans to give you hope and a future.* Then you will call on me and come and pray to me, and I will listen to you. You will seek me and find me when you seek me with all your heart. I will be found by you," declares the LORD, "and will bring you back from captivity. I will gather you from all the nations and places where I have banished you," declares the LORD, "and will bring you back to the place from which I carried you into exile." (verses 4–7, 10–14)

This promise, the one that hangs on plaques in our homes, was not just something said to God's people on a regular day as they worked the fields or went about their lives. It wasn't even something said under healthy or happy circumstances. God's people were exiles in Babylon. They'd been captured, but God promised they wouldn't stay there. He promised to give them hope and a future. And He did. Seventy years

later, just as He promised, the words of the Lord spoken by
Jeremiah came true. Cyrus, king of Persia, came to rule and
issued this decree:

> The LORD, the God of heaven, has given me all the
> kingdoms of the earth and he has appointed me to
> build a temple for him at Jerusalem in Judah. Any of
> his people among you may go up to Jerusalem in Judah
> and build the temple of the LORD, the God of Israel,
> the God who is in Jerusalem, and may their God be
> with them. And in any locality where survivors may
> now be living, the people are to provide them with sil-
> ver and gold, with goods and livestock, and with free-
> will offerings for the temple of God in Jerusalem.[5]

And God's people went home.

*Becky, what are you trying to tell me? How does a story of
exile help my anxious heart? How does telling me that my favorite verse is actually written to a group of exiles help me overcome
my fear that something bad is going to happen to me in the future?* I'm glad you asked . . .

Amid the worst-case scenario, in a time when God's people had turned their backs on Him, He had not turned His
back on them. Even though they deserved to be forgotten
because their relationship with God was contingent on their
obedience, He was still calling to them with hope. He was
still telling them, *I know you forgot who I am, but I have not
forgotten about you. Now use this time to grow. Grow and bless
the place you find yourself in. Bless the people around you, and
know that you won't be in this place forever.*

Sometimes it feels as if God has forgotten about us. It feels as though we prayed and trusted Him and yet we are still facing situations that aren't working out the way we wanted them to or that threaten our peace or security. Sometimes we look around and think, *This sure doesn't look like I thought it would, God. I sure don't feel the way I wanted to in this season of life, God. How did I get here? How do I get out of here?*

And sometimes God asks us to trust Him with the in-between seasons of our lives. He asks us to trust Him with our futures, even when we cannot see how they are going to unfold. He asks us to take His knowledge of tomorrow and use it to imagine a future where He frees us, where He has only good for us, and where our circumstances don't look the way they do right now.

So, I need to ask you some questions: Have you believed the lie that the Lord abandons you and doesn't come through for you? Have you believed the lie that a future exists where He isn't good and His plans for you aren't good? Are you in a place now where you want to trust Him but you can't see how this is all going to unfold in a way that will reveal His kindness or love for your family?

I can almost hear the hearts of so many hurting women who feel as though they are exiles, led away from what they were promised, and who cannot imagine a future where God redeems their situations. I can almost hear women saying to the Lord, *You led me here! God, You asked me to pray for a family, and I am having miscarriages. I'm afraid there will be more, and my heart cannot handle it!* Or *God, You told me to pray for my marriage, but I don't see anything changing! My husband isn't interested in working on healing, and it all feels hopeless. Or God, You brought me to this job or this town or this ministry, but I am looking toward the future and I don't see You in it! God, I peer into the future as far as I can see, and I just can't see Your goodness.*

Friend, you have a powerful imagination. You were designed to look forward and create dreams and plans and a future in your heart that you aim toward. But we must be so careful not to trust our imaginations more than we believe God's promise. We don't want to do this, but sometimes it just happens. We don't want to imagine fire sweeping down the street or a pregnancy that ends prematurely or a divorce or a death. We don't want to believe that God has abandoned us, forgotten about us, or turned away from us. But our hearts can so easily look around at our circumstances and project them forward.

The freeing news is that we have a God who says in the midst of all our suffering and discouragement, *I have hope and a future for you! Don't look around here and believe this is all there is to see!*

DON'T USE YOUR IMAGINATION TO CREATE A WORST-CASE SCENARIO.

Don't use your imagination to create a worst-case scenario. If God can pursue the Israelites even in their disobedience, if He can call to them through His prophet and send them a letter letting them know that in the end it will all be okay because He still loves them and has a future for them, then how much more can He call to us today?

If the Lord can see the good future He has for His people, even when they are in the middle of Babylonian captivity, then surely we can see God's good future for us on the other side of the Cross. After the sacrifice of Jesus, which made a way for us to have direct access to God Himself, how much more can we trust that He hasn't turned His back on us or forgotten about us?

God sent a letter to His people, saying, *Wait! It looks like the end of your story, but it's not. My plans are still to prosper you. So, what I need you to do is grow well in this place, even when you don't understand why you're here or what I'm doing!* Therefore, surely we can believe the scripture that comes much later, after Jesus has already overcome hell and the grave, where Paul tells us,

No eye has seen, no ear has heard,
    and no mind has imagined
what God has prepared
    for those who love him.[6]

I know I am repeating myself here, but I want this to settle deep into your heart. There is no future where the Lord doesn't show up for us. There is no future where He doesn't come through for us. And the minute we begin to look toward the future as He does, the minute we begin to use our creative minds to imagine a world where tomorrow is full of hopeful expectation, then it doesn't matter what it looks like all around us. It doesn't matter if all we can see is a threat. The Lord can see the truth, and He has given us the ability to see tomorrow through His eyes.

So, I want you to pull your most recent fear to the front of your mind. What is it? What have you been imagining? Have you imagined the future and your marriage fails? Your children do not love you? You don't make it? You don't have enough money? You are all alone? You are outcast or abandoned? It's all your fault? You don't reach the goal? The fire destroys everything? Let's take those thoughts and exchange them. Let's imagine the Lord walking with us in the garden even as we make our way through this forest of fear. Let's imagine tomorrow with the Lord.

Let's Pray Together

Place your hand on the top of your head and say these words with me:

Father, I trust You. I trust that it's going to be okay. I pray Your Word over my mind now. I break down every proud thought that puts itself against Your wisdom. I take hold of every thought and make it obey You. I trust that You will come for me, Lord. I trust that the thing I'm most afraid of happening is something You have already seen worked out for my good. You already have a strategy to walk me through it and overcome it. You have a good future for me. I trust that You will meet me tomorrow and that You are with me today.

Help me recapture my imagination. Help me imagine today and tomorrow full of Your presence only. And when my imagination wants to run away with me, help me grab it and recommission it to see only the future You have in Your heart for me. I ask in Jesus's name. Amen.

SAY THIS WITH ME

There is no future where God's love doesn't come to my rescue. I believe His promise to give me hope and a future. I will trust Him!

TRY THIS

You have likely used your imagination to create a worst-case scenario. Close your eyes and practice imagining a future where God meets you and comes through for you in the areas of your life that presently feel uncertain.

7

Face the Wolf

· · · · · · · · · · · · · · · · · · ·

HOW AVOIDANCE AFFECTS OUR ANXIETY

I t was another sweltering August in Oklahoma, and I had decided to wear jeans for the first day of seventh grade at my brand-new school. This is a decision many Oklahoma students make year after year, even though the temperature can be upwards of 110 degrees when school goes back into session. Blue jeans are just part of the uniform of agricultural life. This, however, was not why I chose to wear them. I, Becky Thompson (well, Becky Pitts at the time), the citiest of all city girls, who had never seen a cow or pig in person, decided to wear jeans on the first day of seventh grade because they made me feel big. In hindsight, that was probably the last year of my life when feeling big was the goal.

My dad was the new Methodist preacher in a very small town that year. It was a "blink while driving and you'll miss it" kind of small town. Truthfully, the town was small, but I felt smaller. I guess when I think about it, I've always felt small. And I don't just mean in size. I suppose I have always felt at least a little intimidated and unsure of myself.

The in-between phase I found myself in that summer was the worst. I was in between my old city life and this new life in the country. I was in between elementary and high school. And worst of all for my confidence level, I was in between clothing departments. I was in that awkward stage of being too small to wear clothes from the juniors' section but too old to want to wear what fit from the kids' department. Basically, I was a junior high girl stuck in a fourth grader's body, forced into wearing character T-shirts and rainbow-colored shorts in a brand-new town. As you might understand, I had some uncertain feelings about the first day of seventh grade.

As I waited for school to start that summer, I imagined entire scenarios where I'd walk into a classroom and the other kids would gather and whisper about how little and awkward I was.

Did you see the new girl? Ugh. How old is she? Why is she even here?

Of course, these conversations never actually happened, but those imaginations of ours can be powerful and can get the best of us. Can't they?

I wasn't going to be a joke if I could help it. So, imagine my pure joy that summer when I discovered that jeans from the juniors' department finally fit. I think they were a size 00, but they did not have pink stitching on the pockets, and I was basically finally an adult.

The morning of the first day, I completed my outfit with an Old Navy T-shirt, white Adidas with pale blue stripes, and caked-on blue glitter eyeshadow. I felt about as big as I could (for actually feeling so tiny and insignificant and alone).

I climbed into our red-orange 1973 Malibu, which had been given to my family as a gift when one of our cars had broken down earlier that summer and we couldn't afford to replace it. It smelled like exhaust, and whereas most vehicles have fabric or leather upholstery on the seats, this one had green porch carpet. It was the ugliest thing, but for whatever reason, I wasn't embarrassed by it. My daddy drove it with the windows down (probably because of the exhaust fumes and the fact that the air conditioner didn't work), but I was too nervous about the day to notice that I should probably be embarrassed. Those jeans were giving me confidence.

He pulled up to the school, where my happy classmates walked inside in pairs. Everyone had grown up together. Everyone had a best friend. Everyone except me. I looked over at my dad, and he reminded me that there were only a few hours until lunchtime.

The school had an open-campus policy, which meant you couldn't drive to lunch but you could go as far as your legs could carry you. Luckily for me, my daddy didn't drive me to school that morning because we lived far away. He drove me because he's the type of dad who wouldn't let his little girl face the first day alone. I'd be able to walk home for lunch as often as I wanted.

All morning, I anchored my heart into that hope. *Just a few more hours and I can walk home to our little house and the red metal farm table in the kitchen. My parents will have food waiting for me, and it will feel familiar and safe. Just a few more hours to go. I can do this.*

As the lunch bell rang and I made my way toward my house, every part of me that celebrated those jeans that morning immediately regretted wearing them. The half mile wasn't far, but with the August sun beating down on my back at midday, I was dead by the time I walked through the back door of our little house. All the way dead. Writing-this-from-heaven dead. It was the hottest day of the year. Don't look that up to see if I'm right because it's probably not true. But it felt like the hottest day of the year, and my jeans made it miserable.

Red-faced, exhausted, and sweating right through those size 00 pants, I collapsed into a chair in the kitchen. My momma had a sandwich for me on the table, but I couldn't possibly think about eating. I just wanted to drink something cold and pretend I didn't have to go back to that school ever again. Except I did, and I would every day.

Can I tell you something kind of sad? I walked home for lunch every day that year, wearing jeans as often as they were clean. I never once stayed at school to eat lunch in the cafeteria, and it wasn't because I preferred my momma's cooking or wanted to torture myself with those blistering hot walks back to my house. It was because I was terrified of the cafeteria.

What's so scary about the cafeteria? Just about everything, if you really want to know. The thought of walking into a room and trying to find a place to sit made me physically ill. So many people! So many opportunities for something to go wrong! It seems so simple, doesn't it? Get a tray from the lunch line, carry it to an open seat, eat, dump the tray, go back to class. But for me, it was more than that. It was much worse than that! It was a daily opportunity for rejection. *What if I can't find a place to sit? What if no one talks to me?*

What if other people notice that I can't find a place to sit and that no one wants to talk to me? To cope with the anxiety that came up in my chest each day around noon, I just avoided it all.

Did you know that avoidance is one of the most common symptoms of an anxiety disorder? Avoidance can be what we do or don't do to keep ourselves from experiencing negative emotions. Avoidance is simply the choice not to expose ourselves to what causes us to feel afraid. Anxiety might cause us to avoid germs or crowds or avoid answering phone calls, reaching out to that mom who says she wants to get a coffee, doing laundry, doing dishes, or making decisions. Basically, anything that triggers anxiety can also trigger avoidance in those who struggle.

For me, I walked home for lunch every day, rain or shine, snow or wind, because being hot or cold or wet or miserable was the price I was willing to pay not to feel emotionally uncomfortable around other people who might not like me, accept me, or include me if I dared to go into the cafeteria. I walked home and ate alone so I could avoid the anxious and unwanted feelings of being rejected or left out. I made choices to protect my heart, even when they didn't make much sense to anyone else, because that's what anxiety compelled me to do. And to be honest, I wore jeans on the hottest days of the year for the same reason I walked home each day at lunch. I was willing to sacrifice my physical comfort to ensure my emotional well-being, all while mentally spiraling out in daily panic.

Does any of this sound familiar? I obviously don't mean the jeans or the cafeteria or the walking home. I mean at some point in your life, has anxiety ever caused you to pull back to avoid rejection or intimidation or fear? Does anxiety ever manifest itself in this way for you now?

Stop and consider for just a second whether feelings of nervousness ever cause you to want to shut the door on entire areas of your life. Does anxiety ever make you think, *Nope! Can't do it. Can't go in there. Let's just act like I don't ever have to.* This could be a figurative door you want to close, such as avoiding a situation or conversation that will make you feel uncomfortable. Or it could be a literal door, such as the door to the spare bedroom where I keep my clean laundry that needs to be folded or the door to my office, for example.

Nothing in either room is scary. Nothing will cause me harm. I don't have a bear trapped in the spare bedroom or an octopus in the office. But certain things in each room cause me to feel anxious. I've avoided doing the laundry for so long that when I finally washed and dried it all, I just didn't have time to put it away. My daily schedule and the demands I'm facing currently keep me from completing some daily tasks that absolutely pile up if I don't stay on top of them.

Often I just can't maintain everything that's asked of me. I feel as though a giant wave is going to overtake me and I cannot afford to pause and rest. So, rather than do little bits of the laundry and slowly catch up, I want to just shut the door so I don't have to look at it. I want to go into the room when I need clean socks or pajamas or whatever the kids need, but I don't want to have to walk by the open door every day as the laundry seems to shout, *Hey, Becky! You can't keep up with your life, and you're never going to make it!* Obviously, the laundry doesn't have a voice, but if it did, that's what it would say. In reality, avoiding the laundry actually makes the situation worse.

The same is true for my office. Did I mention that I'm not writing this book from some cabin in the mountains or by the beach, even though they're only about an hour's drive from where I live? I mean, hopefully at some point during the penning (typing) of this manuscript, I can find a minute to slip away from my family. But for now, it's 10:29 on a Tuesday night, and I'm sitting in my office while everyone else sleeps.

Don't picture an Instagram office either. You know, with cute built-ins and shiplap or a hand-painted navy desk inspired by one of those online influencers. It's just a regular room with a place to write and a few extra chairs and bookshelves. And though I have a desk, I'm not sitting at it right now. No, for about a month, my desk has been full of clutter, including papers, letters, and bills that make me too anxious to open them.

The pile of all the things I'm avoiding was moved to the floor, and then over the course of time, it spread across the room. To be honest, there is clutter on just about every surface of this small space. It's not because I'm naturally messy, even though if you asked my college roommates, they'd disagree. It's because when I'm anxious, my house tells on me. Simple things like going through the mail or listening to voice mails or answering texts can feel overwhelming when I procrastinate. Then too much time goes by or the pile grows too big and I want to avoid it because what if I missed something important and then I have to deal with it? Ugh. Just typing this makes me feel panicky.

So, here I sit, surrounded by letters, school papers, sign-ups I was supposed to send back to school but missed, insurance statements that could probably just go through the shredder since they're all available online, and advertisements that came in the mail for 20 percent off an oil change at a place I've never heard of. I've got my kids' artwork in a stack and receipts I really don't need and cords to who-knows-whose tablet or game system. I've got stamps and Sharpies aplenty. I've got paper clips and staples galore. You want pay stubs? I've got twenty. But who cares? No big deal. Pile on mooooore.

The point is, those of us with anxiety-induced avoidance avoid what makes us nervous. And then often that avoidance worsens the situation. The piles of mail grow. The dishes stack up. The friendship gets a little awkward because we aren't answering the calls, and then our anxiety about not responding makes us avoid the friend altogether. Do you see how avoidance can make what we are afraid of come true?

Here's a situation that took place a few years ago. A friend of mine sent me a simple text message offering to take care of something for me. I needed to really consider how I wanted to answer the message because I was going to tell her I didn't want her to do what she was offering. It seemed as though the answer should be easy, but I needed to tell her why I was answering the way I was. I didn't want my answer to make our friendship awkward.

Because I didn't have time to type out my full response while my kids were climbing all over me, I decided I'd wait until I could answer properly. After I finally got the kids to bed, I picked up my phone, but it was too late to send a message. I didn't want to bother my friend in the middle of the night, so I promised myself I would reply first thing in the morning. You probably know what happened. Morning came, afternoon came, evening came, and when I finally had a free second to answer, it was too late again.

What my friend didn't know was that a dozen stressful situations were unfolding in my personal life and my days were all blurring together. The anxiety was terrible, and I was already a hot mess. The time that had passed since her text was making things worse. And if that wasn't bad enough, she sent a follow-up message. It was something like a simple "Hello? Just making sure you got my message." But it was as if she said, *Becky, I feel like you're avoiding me. Don't you like me? Did I do something wrong? Are you a good friend?*

I couldn't possibly know what she was actually thinking when she sent that text, but anxiety convinced me I did. I had even more explaining to do now. I had to explain why I was answering her the way I was and why I hadn't answered. And I had to try to convince her that my decline of her invitation and the subsequent silence had nothing to do with each other. But I couldn't. It was too big and too hard. So I avoided her. I didn't answer when she called. I didn't reply to the text message. I just avoided the whole situation. And the avoidance compounded the problem by a bajillion.

Here's the worst part. I had to see this person face to face because we were both going to attend a common event. Ugh! And rather than just go up to her and come clean about how the anxiety I was experiencing had caused me to completely flake on our friendship, I just pretended she wasn't in the room. The fear of being misunderstood in the very beginning, together with the avoidance of the conflict, created the very conflict I was afraid of and then caused my friend to misunderstand me.

While avoidance is one of the most common coping behaviors, I have personally found that it usually ends up reinforcing the fear. I suppose that makes sense, though. It's hard to remove the fear in our lives when we are busy avoiding it.

The desire to hide from or avoid what makes us afraid is as old as time itself. Hiding is a consequence of the fall of humanity. Think back to the garden again. (Yes . . . *again.*) When Adam and Eve sinned, Scripture says their eyes were opened. They realized they were naked, and what did they do? The immediate action Adam and Eve took after they sinned was to sew fig leaves together to cover their nakedness and hide from God. Genesis 3:9–10 says,

The LORD God called to the man, "Where are you?"
He answered, "I heard you in the garden, and I was afraid because I was naked; so I hid."

MAYBE BRAVERY ISN'T DOING HARD THINGS EASILY. MAYBE TRUE BRAVERY IS DOING HARD THINGS EVEN WHEN THEY'RE NOT EASY.

This is still humanity's natural response when we feel afraid today. It is just that simple. But how do we stop retreating? How do we overcome our programmed desire to avoid what makes us feel afraid? Eventually, if we are going to overcome it, we have to face it. And maybe that's the bravest thing of all. Maybe bravery isn't doing hard things easily. Maybe true bravery is doing hard things even when they're not easy. You're braver than you know, friend. You can face your fear.

Whatever You Do, Don't Run

Not long ago, I was in my kitchen setting the table for dinner when my daughter walked in and told me, "Mom! Did you know that if you're face to face with a wolf, you're not supposed to run?" I'm sure you've experienced those times in motherhood when your kid wants to tell you about a video game or some unfairness with his sibling or something that has nothing to do with anything at all and you are completely gone. He's talking and you're doing your absolute best to make sure he can't tell you're not there. Inside, you're thinking about what you need from the store later, that funny meme your friend sent you, or how guilty you should feel about disliking every part of this moment in your day. I was zoned out as my daughter, Kadence, came into the room, but for some reason her comment snapped me out of my mommy haze.

"Say that again," I requested.

"When a wolf comes at you, you're not supposed to run. Whatever you do, Momma, don't run! You're supposed to stand big and try to make them think you're scarier than they are."

Her words sent an electricity through my spirit. It was as if instantly I saw two things—the wolves in my life and how I had not done a very good job of standing my ground.

I think plenty of wolves roam in the forest of fear. They are taunting intimidators that seem to circle us and make us retreat. These wolves are the anxieties and worries that show up out of nowhere, and when they do, often the first response is, "Run!" Everything says, "Hide!" But what if we stood our ground or even advanced to regain what we'd lost?

My daughter's words rang in my ears. "Stand big. . . . You're scarier than they are."

Fascinated by this, I did a little reading on wolves, mostly because I wanted to see if what she had seen on the educational television show was accurate. I have no plan of running into any wolves in real life (again, see chapter 5), but I was curious whether there was any more to this analogy.

I found an article on *Business Insider* that featured the advice of Oliver Starr, who raised wolves and worked with a Yellowstone wolf reintroduction program. Starr advised using your jacket or shirt to make yourself seem taller or bigger than you actually are. He said to make loud noises but to avoid sounding afraid. Starr suggested using sticks, rocks, or any nearby weapon if you can reach it without making yourself vulnerable. But the advice that keeps playing over and over in my heart is this: never turn your back on a wolf, and "whatever you do, don't run. Wolves are what is known as coursing predators meaning they take their prey on the run. If you watch wolves hunt you'll immediately see this in action. Wolves will attempt to get the animals they prey upon to run. If they don't run wolves usually don't pursue the attack."[1]

Did you catch that? *If wolves' prey don't run, the wolves usually won't pursue the attack.* Friend! Isn't that just like the Enemy of our hearts? He wants us to run. He wants us to hide. He wants us to turn our backs and pretend that whatever we are afraid of isn't there. But when we do, it quite often overtakes us! The avoidance makes it all worse.

IF WE LOOK FEAR IN THE FACE AND REFUSE TO GIVE IN TO IT, THE ENEMY LOSES HIS POWER.

But we are stronger than the wolves! We are bigger than the wolves. If we don't run, if we don't avoid, if we look fear in the face and refuse to give in to it, the Enemy loses his power.

Maybe your anxiety is triggered by social situations. You are lonely and want to be accepted, but you avoid reaching out to other moms or accepting their invitations because you want to protect yourself from those anxious feelings. Anxiety points toward some corner and says, *You'd better go hide over there so you don't have to experience that terrible pain of being unwanted.* And we trust it. We trust that anxiety is just protecting us from an uncomfortable outcome. And so before we even have the chance to see how it will turn out, we tell ourselves these moms wouldn't really like us anyway so we should just stay away. We turn our backs, and then the Enemy says, *Why doesn't anyone love you? Why can't you make friends? It's because something is wrong with you!* Gross, gross lies!

So, what if we faced that fear instead? The truth is, to overcome certain fears, we must want whatever is on the other side of our fear more than we want to protect ourselves from feeling afraid. Read that again and process it for just a second. We must want the friendships more than we want to protect ourselves from rejection. We must want to be caught up on the laundry more than we want to avoid feeling anxious about how much there is to do. We must want to experience life more than we want to protect ourselves from the potential dangers of going into public places. We must want to take back the power we have given our fear more than we want to avoid it and pretend it doesn't exist.

This is why professional counselors are so important. Yes, we have the Holy Spirit, whom Scripture tells us is our comforter and counselor. But sometimes the Holy Spirit leads us right into a licensed therapist's office, where we can find practical tools to face the fear in our lives rather than run from it. We can learn strategies to face what we are avoiding. We can be handed sticks to throw at the wolves in our lives. We can learn what we need to shout or do to cause our fears to disengage. There is so much value in pursuing advice from those who can help us remove fear's power by refusing to run from what we so desperately want to avoid.

"Whatever you do, Momma, don't run!"

It really is powerful advice.

LET'S PRAY TOGETHER

Father, sometimes all we want to do is hide. We want to avoid facing our fear and give away more of our peace as a result. Help us, Lord. Help us face our fears, knowing You have already overcome them. Be our counselor and help us find the right professionals who can strategically give us the tools to disarm what is causing our anxiety.

You have a strategy for each of us. You have freedom for us. And we thank You in advance for helping us be bigger than our fear because You are bigger than anything we will face. You said, "He who is in you is greater than he who is in the world."[2] We will stand on that truth today. We ask in Jesus's name. Amen.

SAY THIS WITH ME

God is going to help me face what is causing me anxiety so I can overcome what would try to intimidate me. My days of avoidance are ending, and I'm coming out of hiding.

TRY THIS

················

Make a list of the situations, people, responsibilities, or tasks that you have been avoiding. What is one practical way that you can face these wolves in your life?

8

Raccoons and Other Scavengers

HOW TO PROTECT YOUR PEACE AT ALL COSTS

I have been camping only once in my life. I would take more time to explain this, but I feel like I covered it with the whole "I don't hike/run" discussion we had earlier. You get it. So, imagine my pure delight when my husband told me shortly after we arrived in Los Angeles that he had signed us up for our church's annual family camp. I mean, I get it. He's on staff at the church. Staff was highly encouraged to attend, and it would be a good way to connect with other families. We had to go. But we didn't really have to go. But it would be a good idea if we went. Except would it really? Are you catching the internal struggle I dealt with here?

I mean, there really was no getting out of it, so I figured we might as well just jump in fully and enjoy it. And by we, I mean my husband. He got the tent and the little gas grill we could use to cook our family's meals. He went on Amazon and ordered blow-up mattresses, sleeping bags . . . all of it. The registration was free, but it cost a cool couple of hundred to get prepared for this thing. By the time we pulled out of the driveway, the back of our minivan was *loaded*. So much gear.

Of course, as the momma with anxiety, I did my own preparing. I prepped our first aid kits and made sure we had all the medicine we might need. I made some meals ahead of time that we could simply reheat. I looked up the closest hospital to the campground. I researched safe temperatures for storing food and verified that our ice chest wouldn't spoil our food and give us food poisoning in the forty-eight hours we were out in the wilderness. I mean, Jared got us prepared, but I feel as though I got us *really ready*. Do you know what I mean? Of course you do. You're a mom. You get it.

The day of the camping trip came, and we made the drive to the beautiful El Capitán State Beach campground. I had been promised ocean views and a retreat from the city life that was such a contrast to the wheat fields I had recently left behind in Oklahoma. We turned down Highway 1, which is known as the Pacific Coast Highway, and we had hills on our right and gorgeous ocean on our left. The kids were in relatively good moods, and I kept thinking, *Maybe this whole camping thing isn't going to be nearly as bad as I thought.*

That's when we exited the highway and pulled into the campground. I didn't see a quiet road winding down to where we'd be sleeping. No. Nope. Nuh-uh. There was the highway, the parking lot for our group camping site, and then the tent area. From the place where we'd sleep that night, we could see the tops of semitrucks driving down the highway. It was far from the majestic beach camp I had been promised by both my husband and the image I'd found online.

As a matter of fact, it was pretty much the worst. And if the proximity to the highway wasn't bad enough, a train track lay in front of our campsite, complete with a commuter train that ran between the highway and the parking lot every hour (and blew its horn as it roared through camp). Oh, and a damaged chain-link fence stretched behind us, which was the only thing preventing my children from plummeting off the hill and falling to the rocky beach below.

I mean, it was just about the worst situation for a person who struggles with anxiety: normal camping worries compounded by the highway, the ocean, and the train. But I will say this: as we set up our tent and the kids found their friends from church, it was a lot more fun than I thought it would be . . . well, until night came.

After playing hard all day, the kids fell asleep quickly. I was grateful they didn't fuss or wish they were at home or even require all the steps that must be followed when we are going to bed in our house. You know, all the bedtime routines: "sit with me, read me a book, now another book, sing me a song, tell me a story, hold my hand while I fall asleep." Everyone, including my husband, just lay down and went to sleep, which honestly makes me realize we could probably do this simpler bedtime routine at home too. The point is, they went to sleep quickly, and I was the only one left awake.

One by one, lights went out in neighboring tents until I seemed to be the last one awake in the entire campground, listening to the noise all around. After all, we have great hearing as moms. We can hear unauthorized snacks being opened across the house or children whisper-fighting after they were told to get along or separate. We can wake from dead asleep because someone made that one telling gag noise that means we'll be changing sheets at 4:00 a.m. But that night, my momma super senses weren't so appreciated.

I lay there on the sticky plastic air mattress, listening to everything. I could hear the roar of the ocean (and highway traffic). I could hear the wind blowing through the trees above our tent. And I could hear . . . *rattling? Shifting?* As if someone were right outside our tent.

I sat up and shook my husband.

"Jared! Jared. Someone's outside our tent."

He didn't move.

"Jared. Did you hear that?"

Juuh-langity-jang!

Someone was definitely messing with our pots and pans. "Who's out there?" I whispered. My mind raced. *Is it a vagrant walking in off the highway and looking for some food? Or maybe a bad guy with bad intentions who's also interested in grabbing a bag of chips before he acts with ill intent? Do bears live next to the ocean? I mean, I know there's a bear on the state flag, but do they live in this part of the state?* Oh, the things our minds come up with in the middle of the night.

I peered through the small flap of our tent, terrified of what I'd see. We had opened it to let in a breeze that night, but it doubled as a spy hole.

Nothing. Just black night. Just the wind. Just the trees. Just the dark and . . .

Two beady eyes suddenly appeared and stared back at me!

I screamed—shrieked, really—and that was the day I died. All the way dead. I'm writing this from heaven now. Jesus says hello. *So scary.*

No. It was a raccoon. It was actually a group of raccoons, which Google tells me is called a gaze. That night, however, I definitely didn't call them a gaze. Because this book is going to be on Christian bookstore shelves, I won't type out what I called those raccoons in the middle of the night. But I will tell you this: fear has a way of bringing out the junk in us.

Have you ever noticed this? We become stressed, anxious, full of what we dislike, and then those fear-filled feelings spill out on those around us. We are short with our children or spouse. We overreact to simple situations. We say things we would never say otherwise. All because anxiety is like a thief in the night, stealing the peace that should be secure. *Sneaky raccoons.*

I will be honest. The next night, we packed away our trash. We brought our big plastic bin full of food into our zippered tent with us. We took steps to secure our campsite because it was important to do so. And I cannot help but think it is just as important for us to look around our lives and survey what is stealing our peace. We might have to take practical steps to keep those raccoons out of our camp.

Common Thieves

So, let's talk about some things that might be stealing your peace and contributing to your anxiety. Do you know the major offenders?

Do you drink tons of caffeine?

Do you get minimal sleep?

Do you eat loads of processed and chemical-filled foods?

Do you crave sugar and binge on it when you are nervous?

You might have some underlying medical condition that triggers your anxious feelings. You might need the Lord to heal some deep places in your heart. You might need to see a doctor, pastor, or therapist. But, friend, you might need to take a good look around your camp and see where you are leaving yourself vulnerable to things that add to your anxiety. You might need to take practical steps to make sure you aren't contributing to your condition of unrest. Let's discuss some of the most common thieves—specifically how caffeine and lack of sleep can affect our mental health.

When my kids were very young, I was a multiple-cups-of-coffee-a-day-to-survive momma. I would make a pot of coffee as soon as I got up and drink it all morning, heating it up again and again and sometimes forgetting it altogether in the microwave. In the afternoon, I'd grab a Dr Pepper at a drive-through or crack open a can from the fridge. I did not sleep. Ever. My kids were never great sleepers at night. So, caffeine was literally a drug that I used to keep my body going. It was very unhealthy.

One year, I decided I'd give up coffee for Lent (the forty days leading up to Easter). I don't always fast or give up something for Lent, but that year I felt it was something that could really benefit my spiritual walk. So I prayed about what I should set aside for forty days. I wanted to give up something that I would notice, something that would make me turn my heart to prayer every time I felt its absence in my life. And as I was praying, the first thing that came to my mind was coffee.

Get behind me, Satan! was my immediate reaction. But when I really thought about just how much my flesh was depending on caffeine, I saw how much more I'd need the Lord to sustain my strength. It would be the perfect thing to sacrifice for those forty days. I would daily have to rely on the Lord's supernatural provision instead of coffee's temporary help. It would be great. Are you sensing just how much work this would take?

Honestly, once I got past the caffeine headaches from the withdrawals my body experienced, I felt great. I wasn't as exhausted as I thought I would be, and I felt noticeably calmer. Somehow, by some supernatural grace, I even lasted all forty days without any coffee (or even any soda). You should have been there on the day when this momma of two tinies got her first warm cup of coffee in nearly seven weeks once Easter came.

It was pure delight. I made that cup of coffee with love. I held my warm mug. I sipped. I waited for the rush of energy to hit . . . and then something totally bizarre happened. I nearly passed out. Not even thirty minutes after I had drunk about half a cup of coffee, I was standing at my kitchen island, gripping the sides of it. The room was spinning. I felt light headed and dizzy. I was home alone with two very small children, and I felt as if I were going to black out. In a total daze, I grabbed my cell phone and called my mother-in-law, who could be at my house in three minutes.

I slid down onto the floor and called my children over to me. I asked them to sit with me in case I got so drowsy I fell asleep. And I told them to stay right with me until Grams got to the house. I have never felt more out of control. I hadn't lost consciousness when my mother-in-law pulled up just a few minutes later. My kids were sitting on either side of me on the kitchen floor, and the room was still spinning. My heart was racing. My hands were shaking. I couldn't catch my breath, and I was certain I was having a heart attack. It never crossed my mind that the half cup of coffee could have anything to do with my current condition.

The emergency room in our small town was less than a mile down the road, with not a single stoplight or stop sign between my home and the hospital. My mother-in-law helped load up my kids and drove me to the ER. I was seen immediately, and the doctor began to run all the standard tests. He listened to my heart and lungs. He took my vitals. The whole time, I was in a complete daze. My heart raced, and I was sweaty. I was breathing as if I had run too long in gym class without any water on the hottest day of the year (or as though I had walked home in one-hundred-degree heat wearing jeans in the seventh grade). The worst part was that I was sure I was dying. I felt as if my chest were going to explode. In my mind, there was no scenario where this ended well.

That's when the doctor came back into the room and told me I could go home because absolutely nothing was wrong with me medically. I was confused. I felt as though I were dying, and I was supposed to just walk out? What kind of school gave this guy a diploma?

My husband had arrived from work. He looked over at me struggling to breathe and with my face white as a ghost, and I could tell he was just as confused as I was. The doctor continued, "You're just having a panic attack. You will be fine. You are a young mom of young children, and you just need more sleep. You're too stressed, and it caught up with you."

My mouth hung open until I could gather my words. "You think this is all in my head? I'm stressed and so I'm panicked about nothing?" I had no idea how panic attacks work. I didn't know that even when my emotions seemed to be just fine, my body could become so overwhelmed that my nervous system would trigger a full-blown "We are under attack" response. I didn't know that stress can trigger a fight-or-flight response and that my brain would send signals to all the different parts of me to act as if I were in danger, when there was no actual threat. And I had no idea that caffeine had triggered the whole ordeal.

Here's what actually happened in my body. Before I gave up coffee, I had developed a tolerance to high amounts of caffeine. When I removed it from my system and my body began to heal, I was the least anxious I had been in years. It's why the doctor's comments about my episode being a panic attack didn't make any sense to me. "No, I feel really good! I'm not in a bad place at all," I had insisted to him. But with the reintroduction of caffeine, I had immediately sent my body into an anxious tailspin.

The terribly unfortunate truth—and I'm so, so sorry to have to break it to you—is that caffeine can be a huge contributor to the anxiety so many women face. (I can almost picture you with your fingers in your ears, saying, "Nah, nah, nah. I can't hear you!") I know that's not fun news. Caffeine can feel like a mom's lifeline, especially after a long night awake with small children or a sick child or with a big day ahead of her. But caffeine is a powerful drug, and we should take just a minute to look at how it can be stealing your peace.

America's Favorite Drug

We all know caffeine increases your alertness. It wakes you up. It does all the things you expect your morning cup of coffee to do for you. Caffeine is a stimulant that occurs naturally in foods and beverages, and it's the world's most popular drug. While we enjoy it for its stimulating benefits, caffeine and anxiety don't always mix, and it's not because of those caffeine jitters you might get. It's because of what those jitters mean.

To really understand why caffeine might be hurting you, we need to take a closer look at the way it affects your brain. Without getting too deep in the weeds of science, it is helpful to understand a few facts, so hang with me here.

We have something in our bodies called adenosine. Adenosine is responsible for slowing down the nerve activity in your brain and for regulating neurotransmitters such as dopamine. Think of adenosine as the mom who walks into your rowdy brain's room and says *Okay! You all need to calm down in here!* and then acts as a supervisor, making sure everyone does what is supposed to be done.

The only problem is that caffeine molecules look like adenosine molecules.[1] So caffeine binds really easily to adenosine protein receptors. It would be like having the mom's evil twin come into the room and block the doorway to keep the mom out. Where adenosine keeps balance and helps your body stay naturally calm, caffeine locks the door and says, Go wild!

Caffeine then goes to work, increasing brain activity and causing a reaction in your body that mimics the fight-or-flight response. It increases blood flow to muscles. It increases your breathing and heart rate, and it makes you more aware. According to health.com, your body can't really distinguish the effects of caffeine and anxiety: "Restlessness, nervousness, headaches, sweating, insomnia, and ringing in the ears are other common signs of caffeine-triggered anxiety."[2]

The link between caffeine and anxiety is so common that the American Psychiatric Association identifies caffeine-induced anxiety disorder as a recognized disorder.[3] Friend, this is definitely something worth paying attention to. While not everyone responds the same way to caffeine, we should take its potential side effects seriously—especially if we naturally struggle with anxiety.

Are you making a cringing face? I'm making a cringing face, thinking about you reading this. Sweet, sleepy, worn-down momma friend of mine, I know this is not the best news. I get it. I know what it's like to be down-to-the-bone tired, where you just physically cannot move because you are so ridiculously exhausted.

I remember sitting on my couch sobbing one afternoon

when my oldest two were just babies. I was so desperate for a nap. I would have paid all the money in my bank account just to put my head down on my pillow and close my eyes for the rest of the day. But while a nap wasn't possible, caffeine was. Caffeine might be the thread you're hanging on to as well. The anchor of your sanity. The one thing that keeps you from falling asleep while standing in the laundry room, restarting the washing machine for the third time because you just keep forgetting to move those clothes to the dryer before they start to smell again. I get it.

And this is usually where a Bible teacher would pop in and remind you that the grace of Jesus can be your thread, your anchor, the one thing keeping you from falling apart. I'm not going to say that because you already know it's true. God is your strength. Period. I don't need to go through a whole lesson on it this minute.

But I will tell you, sis, that the Lord sees your exhaustion, and I believe He does want to remind you of what we talked about back in chapter 4. He is your wilderness guide, your constant friend, your hope, your source, your ever-present help in time of need. And if you need to give up caffeine as a strategic battle move to protect your heart and reclaim your peace, Jesus loves you enough to help you with that too. He is intimately involved in all your day-to-day activities, and if you need Him to walk with you as you decide to cut the coffee, He's all in.

Listen, here's what it all comes down to. Caffeine might be giving you a boost of energy, but if it is at the expense of your peace, is it worth it? If you are anxious all day long because of the caffeine and then can't sleep at night and then need caffeine the next day to function, how do you break the cycle? You pray, *Lord, give me grace.*

This brings me to my next raccoon in the camp. Let's talk about sleep.

Mom Tired

I don't know if you're like me, but those few hours after my children go to bed are *mine.* I might clean up if it feels important to me to reset my house for the next day. Or I might binge on a few episodes of whatever show I'm into at the time. I might scroll aimlessly on social media, taking in everyone else's lives like the nightly news. I might craft. I might create. I might open a bag of cookies and eat as many as I want without my children staring at me or having to tell them no. Those hours are some of my favorite.

The irony of these hours being my favorite is not lost on me, because most days I am so looking forward to my own bedtime. I wish I could take a nap or rest or just close my eyes for ten minutes. I eagerly await the chance to reconnect my face with my pillow. You know that feeling? But then once the kids are in bed, I'm not thinking about how quickly I can change into my pajamas (if I ever made it out of them in the first place as a stay-at-home mom). I'm thinking, *What am I going to do with all these hours to myself?*

Here's the honest truth. I will fill up those hours. I will stare at my phone and the television, back and forth, consuming all the media I want. And then, when I'm so tired I cannot keep my eyes open one more minute, I will finally go to bed and try to sleep.

This is where I do most of my thinking. I think about life. I think about the day. I replay the whole thing. All of it. I make a note of all the things I think I did well (which never seems to be much) and every area in which I feel as though I fell short (which usually feels like most of it). Guilt can get so loud as I lie there. I worry about my kids. I wonder whether they're going to become God-loving adults. I worry whether I was too stern or not stern enough. I worry about how much screen time they're getting and if they know they are really loved. I wonder if I'm a good enough mom. I think of all the ways I could be better. It's as if this wave of intro-spection washes over me and I just lie there, feeling pretty sure I'm ruining everything. Do you do this too, or is it just me?

This is also where I must go to war against these thoughts. This is where I pray. This is where I ask God to come and speak truth over every lie I'm believing. This is where I must weed out what the Enemy tries to seed into my heart.

It would be great if I could work on all this during the day, but it's when the world goes quiet that my mind raises its metaphorical hand, clears its throat, and says, *Now that I have your full attention, I'd like to discuss some things if you have a minute.* I wrestle with my thoughts and can't sleep, and then I can't sleep because I am worried about not sleep-ing. And this unfortunate cycle of anxiety and lack of sleep and exhaustion continues the next day. Scientists agree that sleep and anxiety go hand in hand, but they have a hard time figuring out which causes which. Is the lack of sleep causing our anxiety, or is the anxiety causing our lack of sleep, or is it both?

So, here's the thing. I know that millions of moms across the world wake up in the middle of the night because they are moms. They wake up because their babies need to be fed or they have sick children. They wake up because someone wet the bed, had a bad dream, or is sleepwalking. They wake up because they are worried about their middle schoolers or teenagers. They wake up and check the clock and then check their phones to make sure their adult children made it home from working the night shift or made it back to their dorm rooms after an event. Moms rarely get consistent nights of great sleep, and unfortunately we cannot often control why we wake up in the middle of the night. But we can at least *sometimes* control how we go to bed.

So, I shared with you my bedtime routine, or lack thereof. What's yours? Do you put your phone away at a certain time? Do you take a calming shower or pray and meditate on God's Word? Do you listen to music or apply essential oils or journal to get yourself ready for sleep?

I hope you said yes! Truly, I hope you did. But maybe you're the momma who lies down with your kid to help her fall asleep and wakes up three hours later, wondering, *What just happened?* You make your way to your room after quickly checking the house, turning out the lights, and making sure the doors are locked. And then you lie there after your weird nap, thinking, *Now what?* Or maybe you enjoy all those hours of mom time to yourself and then plop onto your bed without any prep or winding down.

I know you might be in a season where you have a baby, or you might work the night shift, or you might have some circumstance that causes your bedtime routine to be different from what you'd like it to be. But if you're in a situation where you can do it, setting yourself up for a good night of sleep is important. Regaining the peace of those few hours before bedtime might make the biggest difference in your life.

The National Sleep Foundation says that "ninety percent of people in the US admit to using a technological device during the hour before turning in."[4] The foundation also says that "using electronic devices before bedtime can be physiologically and psychologically stimulating in ways that can adversely affect your sleep."[5] I know so many of us are on our phones right until we go to bed, but we might need to put them away. (Are you reading this on a device before you fall asleep?)

We might also need to be intentional with our own bedtime routines. We know that our kids get cranky when they don't get enough sleep, but what about us? What would you do if you could invest in your mental health before bed? What would you do to keep yourself from going directly from busy day to silent room, where your mind can run wild?

You might need to create a bedtime routine. Perhaps you buy a journal and write out how you are feeling, praying about it as you go. (I know a great one called *My Real Story*, if you're in the market. *Wink, wink.*) Maybe you take a bath or a shower, giving your mind some rest time before your head hits the pillow, so you can work through your thoughts prior to getting into bed. Maybe you read your favorite devotional or your Bible and fill your heart and mind with truth before turning out the light. Will it always be possible? Unlikely. But is it worth considering? Absolutely yes.

As we navigate the forest of fear and walk toward wholeness, we have to make sure we are staying on guard, doing all we can to protect ourselves and our camp from what might steal our peace. So, we might need to give up caffeine and set up healthy bedtime routines. We might need to look at our diets, including our sugar intake and the amount of processed foods we are eating. We might need to make some changes to self-sabotaging behaviors that in the moment simply feel like survival.

Am I saying this will fix you? No. I'm not even saying you need fixing. I am simply saying that while some aspects of anxiety are outside our control, we need to fight for each portion of our peace puzzle that we do have control over. And that might mean giving things up, making some adjustments, and looking very honestly at how different elements of our lives affect our overall mental health. Those raccoons are sneaky, but we can outsmart them, especially if it means protecting our camp.

Let's Pray Together

Father, thank You for helping us realize what the Enemy might use to steal our peace from us. More than anything, we desire to be whole. We desire to live as Your Word says, with the peace of God ruling in our hearts.[6] Help us take practical steps to stop doing things that contribute to our anxiety. Give us wisdom to know what to do. Lead us to the right professionals who can counsel us.

Thank You for this journey of healing. Thank You for walking with us each day. Continue to give us Your wisdom, and bring to our attention anything else that might be stealing our peace. We ask in Jesus's name. Amen.

SAY THIS WITH ME

God cares about all aspects of my life, and He cares about me. He will help me heal and strategize in areas where I've sabotaged my peace and need to fight to defend it. I will listen to His wisdom because I am willing to make necessary changes to benefit my mental health.

TRY THIS

Can you identify the peace-stealing raccoons in your life? Are you consuming too much caffeine? Are you not getting enough sleep? What is one small decision or adjustment you can make today to recapture your lost peace?

9
Sensible Stepping-Stones

....

PRACTICAL METHODS TO INCREASE PEACE

I think my parents just started to expect it. That phone call I would make in the first couple of hours after being dropped off at school. "Is everything okay? Are you all right?" It's hard to describe the anxiety I experienced as a child and the certainty with which I believed something terrible had happened at home while I was away. Everything was always fine. It was just hard to keep focused on learning until I went to the office to call and make sure.

The calls started in the fourth grade. We had just moved to the neighborhood across the street from my elementary school, and my classroom window faced the back of our house. I could see the top two feet of our living room curtains when I got up to sharpen my pencil or turn in a paper at the teacher's desk. At first, I loved feeling so close to home and my parents and everything that felt safe. But one morning, I noticed that the living room curtains were still closed. My mom always opened them when she started her morning activities around the house.

I went back to my desk, and my mind ran wild. *Why are they closed? Is my mom okay? Is she sick? Why hasn't she opened the curtains for the day?* I thought of all sorts of medical issues or bad things that could have happened to her while no one was home to help her. I couldn't take it anymore. I got out of my chair, raced to the teacher's desk, and said, "I need to call my mom right now!"

My teacher looked concerned and asked if I felt sick. When I told her that the curtains were closed and I was sure something was wrong with my mom at home, she sent me back to my desk. I hadn't even thought to come up with an excuse or some lie that would grant me the necessary permission to go to the office and use the secretary's phone. I thought my teacher would be just as worried as I was that something terrible had happened to my mom. She wasn't.

I don't really remember how my fear escalated that morning, but evidently it got to the point that I was finally handed a hall pass. That was the first of many mornings that I'd slip away to make sure everything was okay at home.

As I got older, the calls changed. In middle school, I'd call to make sure my mom was coming to pick me up at the end of the day. In high school, I'd call to make sure I hadn't left my curling iron plugged in. I was and still am "a checker."

While I readily admit that I am currently overcoming (like how I put that?) generalized anxiety disorder, some of my experiences present as symptoms of obsessive-compulsive disorder (OCD) as well. OCD is a mental disorder where people experience obsessive thoughts or compulsions. In my case, I'd obsessively worry to the point of needing to call and make sure everything was okay. I'd have to check and recheck to calm my irrational fears. Do you ever do this? Maybe you check your doors repeatedly before going to bed to make sure they are locked. Maybe you go back into your house to check your hair straightener, even though you know it's off. Maybe you check dosages on your kids' medicine again and again before giving it to them. Maybe you check and recheck the stove to make sure it's really off after cooking a meal. Maybe you check in with friends or family even though you just talked with them, because you're worried about them. Maybe you call to check on your spouse when he doesn't tell you he arrived at his destination safely, because your mind says something terrible has happened.

For some, there is a link between anxiety and OCD. While most of us think of OCD and imagine people who have to repeatedly perform certain behaviors or have everything lined up in a certain order, OCD can actually present as the need to check. Until recently, the handbook used as a guide to diagnose mental disorders, *Diagnostic and Statistical Manual of Mental Disorders*, classified OCD as an anxiety disorder. The most recent edition of this manual moved OCD into its own category of psychiatric conditions. Still, the common link between the two disorders exists.[1]

Interesting, huh? We won't go much into OCD here, but for the sake of this story and the point I'm trying to make, I want to highlight something. A correlation existed between the obsessive worry I experienced and the time of day. In my life now, I notice certain times of the day when my anxiety seems worse. For me, the repetitive thoughts seem to be most prevalent in the first few hours of my day.

If I'm honest, I still wake up with some level of anxiety

most mornings. It doesn't always present as the need to check on my kids or the front door, but some mornings I wake up with racing thoughts and want to check my email or my social media accounts or anyplace where I might discover a terrible situation that needs my immediate attention. My shoulders are tense even after a full night of sleep, and my heart feels stressed first thing in the morning.

So, I have a question for you. Does the anxiety you experience seem to have a schedule? Do you wake up afraid? Do you go to bed anxious? Are you anxious all day long? In the previous chapter, we talked about ways to regain what was taken by peace thieves in our lives, specifically caffeine and poor bedtime routines. In this chapter, it's really important that we look at some proactive steps we can take to increase our peace, beginning with how we start our days.

Start Your Day Right

When you wake up, your hormone levels shift. The levels of melatonin that help keep you in a state of sleepiness drop, while your cortisol levels rise. Cortisol is most known as the stress hormone. It's what our body releases during the fight-or-flight response. It heightens our awareness. It gets our muscles moving, and in the morning, it's part of our bodies' natural process to wake us up and get us going. Studies suggest that cortisol is highest in the first few hours we are awake and it slowly drops throughout the day.[2] Why does this matter?

When we begin our days with this rush of hormones, how can we ensure that we don't become overwhelmed by our bodies' built-in drive to get up and get going? I have a simple plan. We harness this energy to purposefully pursue peace. Think of it like riding a trained horse rather than being dragged by a wild horse.

If that rush in the morning is something you're familiar with, simply knowing that it's coming can relieve some of the anxiety associated with it. Rather than search for a cause when you first open your eyes and feel afraid, remind yourself that your body is simply doing what it's supposed to and that you're going to be okay. Before you reach for your phone, before you walk down the hall to wake up your kids for school, before you even move that toddler foot belonging to the little one who climbed into bed during the night away from your face, say this prayer:

Father, help me focus on Your love, Your truth, and Your presence in my home. Protect my family. Calm my racing heart. Help me use the energy my body has this morning to accomplish what needs to be done. I give today and all its concerns to You. I ask in Jesus's name. Amen.

Focusing our hearts on the Lord first thing in the morning is such an important and yet simple strategy we can take toward gaining peace. The truth is, many of the steps we can take away from fear aren't as complicated as they might seem.

The Right Answer

So, let's talk about some sensible stepping-stones. After all, there are many of them! The internet is full of articles promising anxiety-relieving results, with titles such as "10 Ways to Reduce Anxiety Now," "Try These Five Guaranteed Natural Methods to Cure Your Anxiety," and "These Are the Supplements You Should Be Taking If You Have Anxiety." (For the record, I don't know if these are actual titles of articles, but they are definitely similar to ones I've seen in the past.) It seems as though everyone has something to say or some fast track to peace. As a matter of fact, anytime I mention anxiety online, a few types of well-intentioned people pop in with their solutions. I'm sure you have encountered women like this online as well.

There's the multilevel marketing consultant who says, "I have a drink that is made from natural ingredients. Send me a private message, and I'll tell you how it changed my life." There's the oily momma who chimes in with her go-to combinations of essential oils that have helped her or her customers. There's the exercise momma who reminds everyone that rest, proper hydration, and certain workouts improve physical and mental health. There's the holistic or nutritionist momma who can identify exactly what a person should eat and what supplements she should take to reset and cleanse her body and free it from the toxins contributing to her fear. And there's the momma who has been to a counselor or doctor and is excited to pass along her professional's phone number.

These ladies always seem so eager to share their knowledge. They *know* their methods are the *right* methods. Most of them have used a product or medication, adopted a lifestyle, or taken on healthy habits that changed their lives in some powerful way, and as a result, they are sold out to their solutions. But their persistence is not improperly placed. I applaud all their efforts! They believe in the paths they took to health because they are convinced of the results.

So often I see people complaining online about their friends who seem interested only in selling others a product or lifestyle. But I have to say that if you knew you held the key to free others from fear, you'd likely want to share it too. Right? I mean, if you truly experienced a life-changing result of some product or method, you'd want to help others experience the same freedom. You wouldn't want to watch another person struggle when you know you have the answer.

So, here's what I propose. These friends of ours who have the "right answer" might not have the right answer for us, but they might have just the right answer for someone else. And so we should encourage their efforts because many factors contribute to anxiety and there is more than one way to take a step toward wholeness. There are so many steps, in fact, that we cannot cover them all in this chapter, but we can and will address some of the main bridges that might be helpful as you find your way out of the forest.

Laughter Is the Best Medicine

....

I really love to laugh. No. I mean it. In life, I deeply appreciate and connect with people who enjoy humor. I love comedies over dramas. I laugh at myself often. I think we should all take ourselves so much less seriously than we do. For example, I'm fine with pointing out my own issues or awkwardness. I'm not trying to be unkind to myself, but if I'm in the middle of a conversation and I do something that even I think is a little weird, I stop and say something about it so I and the person I'm talking to can both laugh. Humor is a great bridge to true connection. As a matter of fact, laughter is universal across all languages.

I believe that we should all just laugh more. Moms especially. If ever a demographic of people needed some humor in their lives, right up at the top would be mothers. I mean, basically top of the top. Moms need some laughter therapy.

If you're like me, you probably had no idea laughter therapy is a real thing. It's true, though. You might not know the name Dr. William F. Fry, but this man is known in the scientific community for his research on health and humor.[3] He even coined a new phrase for studying the impact of laughter on health: gelotology. It comes from the Greek word *gelos*, which means "laughter." Fry believed that laughter is as good for your body as exercise is. Studies have gone on to prove Fry correct.[4]

We all know it feels good to laugh, but did you know science is proving that laughter significantly lowers hormones such as cortisol (remember, the stress hormone)? Laughter increases your body's antibody levels. It increases the production of immune cells. It even suppresses pain, and I don't mean just emotional distress. Laughter increases a person's pain tolerance, and it releases endorphins, which help relieve anxiety.[5]

So, here's my question. When was the last time you laughed? I don't just mean chuckled at something your kids did or some meme you saw online. I mean, when was the last time you had a good belly laugh? What if the next time you started feeling totally overwhelmed and hopelessly anxious, you watched your favorite comedian or called that friend who always makes you laugh?

I know it doesn't seem very spiritual, but even God says in His Word that a merry heart is good for us. Solomon, the writer of Proverbs who was known for being a wise man, said, "A merry heart does good, like medicine, but a broken spirit dries the bones."[6] It is so fun to think that thousands of years ago, the Lord showed him what science is proving true. A merry heart and laughter are as good for you as medicine!

The Word of God also says, "The joy of the LORD is your strength."[7] It doesn't say the joy you create by trying really hard is your strength. It says His joy is your strength. So, here's a thought. Maybe the next time you feel anxious, don't just pray for peace. Boldly pray for supernatural joy! What a fun idea! Just as God's love washes over you, imagine God's joy bubbling up inside you.

Remember when you were little and you used to blow into your straw and your drink bubbled up to the top, maybe even splashing over or overflowing your cup? The Bible says God breathed His breath into Adam and Adam became a living being. I keep seeing this picture in my heart as I type of God's blowing His breath into our hearts today and our joy bubbling up. Now, there's a funny picture!

Let's be honest, though: some days, it would take God's supernatural joy to make us laugh. Do you know what I mean? Some days, when our kids are driving us crazy or are skipping their naps or our teens are testing our patience—when everything feels hard and overwhelming—laughing would be a miracle in itself. But if God knows the power of laughter and wants us to have strength, then let's imagine Him blowing His breath into our hearts. Let's imagine Him giving us an infusion of His joy!

The truth is, the challenges we face each day and the lies we believe can seem so big and overwhelming. But what if we laughed at the Enemy? What if we laughed our way through the forest of fear, replacing every anxiety with God's truth and laughing at the darkness rather than hiding from it?

Think of these phrases (or even say them with me). Remember, we aren't laughing at what we are saying. We are laughing at the Enemy, who is trying to stop us from believing them. Ready?

+ God is with me! Ha ha ha!
+ Nothing can get me! Ha ha ha!
+ I'm gonna make it! Ha ha ha!
+ Satan, you don't scare me! Ha ha ha!
+ I've got all I need! Ha ha ha!

+ God's my shelter! Ha ha ha!
+ This will all pass! Ha ha ha!
+ I don't have to be afraid! Ha ha ha!
+ Jesus is going to give me strength! Ha ha ha!
+ My kids have a great mom! Ha ha ha!
+ God is so proud of me! Ha ha ha!
+ I'll make it to the other side! Ha ha ha!

I don't know what your day has been like, but just stop right here and ask the Lord to replace every bit of your anxiety with His joy.

Father, fill my heart now! Overwhelm me with joy that doesn't make sense. Give me Your joy as the strength I need for the rest of today and tomorrow. Help me remember that You desire to produce joy within me. May Your joy in my heart produce laughter in my spirit and even my body! Help me notice the humor around me and Your joy within me. I ask in Jesus's name. Amen.

Take Your Vitamins

Laughter isn't the only stepping-stone we can take toward increasing our peace. Did you know nutrient deficiencies can contribute to our lack of peace? Sometimes gaining ground can be as simple as taking your vitamins. This is something that has changed my life drastically in the last five years.

I first heard of MTHFR while sitting in my perinatologist's office. My husband and I had gone through our second miscarriage, and my OB sent us for more blood work. In addition to discovering that my miscarriages were likely caused by my inability to maintain progesterone levels in early pregnancy, the doctors also discovered a number of other underlying genetic conditions—one of which was an MTHFR mutation. I know; it's a weird abbreviation. According to the US National Library of Medicine, "The MTHFR gene provides instructions for making an enzyme called methylenetetrahydrofolate reductase."[8] You might have caught a part of that word you recognize—*folate*. The MTHFR enzyme is necessary for our bodies to turn folate (vitamin B_9) in our food into L-Methylfolate, which is used for a number of important processes.

MTHFR mutations and pregnancy are often spoken of together, the primary concern being that the mother's body doesn't have the necessary enzyme to process folate and pass that key nutrient on to her baby. It was during my first pregnancy that I learned about and treated my body for the effects of the MTHFR mutation. But it wasn't until about a year after my youngest child was born that I went on to do my own research about how an MTHFR mutation might affect my body in other ways.

So, here's how this works. *Grabbing chalk and putting on science teacher hat* . . . No, wait. Science teachers wear coats. *Putting on science teacher coat* . . . Okay. The MTHFR gene allows our bodies to turn the folate in our food into L-Methylfolate. Our bodies use L-Methylfolate to convert something inside us called homocysteine into methionine.

Our bodies then use methionine to do a lot of important work involving neurotransmitters, and the neurotransmitters play a huge part in our brains' health and activity.[9]

I know you're intelligent and able to follow along, but just in case all these ridiculous words and chemical processes are confusing, here's a breakdown:

1. MTHFR produces the enzyme needed to turn folate in food into a form of the vitamin our bodies can use—L-Methylfolate.
2. L-Methylfolate helps our bodies convert the amino acid homocysteine into another amino acid, methionine.
3. Our bodies then use methionine as part of a process that produces neurotransmitters.[10]

I realized that my body's inability to properly process folate might actually be contributing to the anxiety I've experienced all my life. Crazily, one study suggests that up to 40 percent of the population has some form of MTHFR mutation.[11]

It was a happy day for me when I discovered that companies make daily vitamins with L-Methylfolate in them. This means that this nutrient doesn't need to be converted by my body. It is already in the form my body can absorb. They call vitamins like these bioavailable nutrients. (That's just a fun bonus fact.)

Why am I telling you all this? Do I think you have a genetic disorder that is affecting your mental health? I don't know, and neither do you unless you've been checked for it. That's the point. What we ingest into our bodies and the nutrients our bodies need to thrive shouldn't be an afterthought. An important step we can take toward peace is contacting our doctors to make sure we aren't overlooking a disorder or even an underlying condition such as a nutritional deficiency that could be contributing to our anxiety.

Anxiety is much more complex than just the fear we face, friend. I hope you're feeling empowered to take some important steps for your health. Which brings me to my next point.

Move It or Lose It

Yesterday on my way to church, I turned around and looked at my kids in the back seat. (It's okay. My husband was driving.) I asked them if they had ever heard the word *hypocrite*. I had just read a quote from Robert Murray McCheyne that said, "It is the mark of a hypocrite to be a Christian everywhere except at home."[12] This quote had struck me, and it seemed important to discuss with my kids.

So, we took some time as a family to talk about what the quote meant. We talked about how home is a safe place to express how we really feel, but sometimes that means our families get the not-so-great parts of us. We act at home in ways we'd never act in public because we can be our authentic selves. While we often hold in our real thoughts or feelings everywhere else and make sure we look good to other people, at home we let everything go and share our worries and fears and insecurities.

As their momma, I told my kids that we want to make sure we are honest about how we feel at home. I told them our house is a safe place to be who they really are without being afraid they won't be loved. But we talked about making sure we ask God to help us with all our feelings, inviting Him into our everyday lives.

I could pull a few great nuggets from this conversation, but the reason I share it with you now is because sometimes when authors write books, they don't really let their readers all the way in, even when they're trying to be vulnerable. It makes sense for authors to highlight what they really know and not admit to the areas where they still need growth.

So, in an effort to be authentic "here at home" with you, I need to tell you that this next bit of information is an area in which I'm not an expert by any means. Because I haven't lived this out myself, I almost feel disqualified from sharing these facts with you. Saying "Here's a step you could take to be less anxious" makes me feel like a hypocrite since I haven't walked this bridge or tested this method for myself.

But as I write, I feel the Lord reminding me again and again that you and I are on this journey together. I'm not writing from the other side of anxiety. Most days I'm in it with you. Some days as I've typed these words, I've had to stop, pray, get ahold of my emotions, and wait for my heart to quit racing before I could keep sharing. So, because we are on this journey together, here is something we both might need to do to take a step toward peace. Literally.

Exercise.

You already know that I don't move my body as often as I should. I have made it clear that I don't run. I don't hike. And I dislike the short walk to pick up my kids from school. It's just the way I am. Maybe you aren't like me at all. Maybe you already have a great workout routine. If you do, then what I'm about to tell you is just a reminder of why you should keep it up! But if you are like me, here's some info that might get you—and me—up and moving.

Did you know exercise has many of the same benefits as antianxiety medication? It's true. When you exercise, your body releases endorphins. Endorphins interact with neurotransmitters, the chemicals in your brain, to create a natural painkiller type of response. This affects your mood and mental state.

Exercise also increases your body's serotonin level. Serotonin is one of the neurotransmitters widely associated with depression and anxiety, and although not entirely accepted by everyone in the scientific community, many theorize that low serotonin is linked in some way to anxiety disorders. As a result, doctors often prescribe a type of medication that targets serotonin levels. However, exercise has been known to increase serotonin levels in a way that is similar to the effects of these medications. Even small amounts of exercise result in both immediate and long-term benefits to a person's mental health. I suppose we can agree that if we could increase these levels naturally—with or without the use of medicine as well—it would be worth our efforts. Yes?

According to the Anxiety and Depression Association of America, "In one study, researchers found that those who got regular vigorous exercise were 25 percent less likely to develop depression or an anxiety disorder over the next five years."[13]

So, may I say something about this quickly, mom to mom? First, if you work out, just hang on and let me say something to the momma who doesn't have time, okay? If you're not her, listen to what you might need to share with a friend.

If you're reading this and you do not work out, I know what you might be thinking: *Just what I need. Someone telling me something that I really need to do but that I just don't have time for.* Girl, I get it. I know you might not have much time. You're a mom. I'm not talking to a group of adults with unlimited time. The baby might be throwing a fit, your anxiety might be skyrocketing, and the last thing on your mind is how to strap that little one into a stroller so you can get in a quick jog. I know the only running you might do is running your kids to their next practice. You might work, and you might have a million things on your plate that prevent you from taking good care of yourself. I understand because I'm just like you.

But I have this friend who wakes up every morning and takes turns with her husband hitting the gym. She goes first, comes back, showers, and starts getting her kids ready for school. And in my mind, I love the idea of doing what she does, but practically, I just have no idea how to make that work. I'm usually up late working because of the way life is right now with our family's schedule. So, early morning workouts aren't a possibility for me. And you're not supposed to work out right before bed because exercise wakes up your body and gets it going, and then it can be difficult to sleep.

So, maybe like you, I wonder how I'm supposed to fit it in. I want to offer this suggestion for both of us: let's not overcomplicate it. Maybe each day is different. Maybe while the baby is happy, we take a walk. Maybe while the littles are napping, we do a living room exercise. Maybe when the kids are at school, we take a jog around the neighborhood. And maybe on the days we can, we take it up a notch and get up before everyone else and start the day with healthy hearts and minds.

As I said in the beginning, I've never written a book to a woman who couldn't be my friend, so it's important to tell you that I know how hard this might sound and how impractical it might seem to add something to your day when you are already stretched thin. But studies show that even ten minutes of exercise can improve your mental health. Friend, you are worth those ten minutes. You just are. We just are.

So, another question. Do you have a friend you could call to join you at the park while the kids play and you do a jungle gym workout? Do you have a friend who would wake up and put her little ones in a stroller and run with you for ten minutes in the morning? Do you have someone who could sit with your kids while you run to the gym for thirty minutes? Do you have fifteen minutes in your day currently dedicated to scrolling through social media that you could instead give to an in-home workout that would benefit your mental health?

Practical steps are some of the most necessary when we feel overwhelmed. So, two things. First, take a second to brainstorm how you can move your body for ten minutes today. Second, if you already have a workout routine, think for just a minute about which friend you could invite to join you at the gym or your home. Each intentional step is the most important step we take toward peace.

LET'S PRAY TOGETHER

Father, thank You for caring about each step of our journeys toward wholeness. Thank You for showing us practical steps we can take to improve the way our minds and bodies feel. Lord, help us find not only Your joy to give us strength but also Your wisdom to know how to schedule our days so we can get moving and exercise. Will You please give us insight into what we should do next? Your Word says, "The steps of a good man are ordered by the LORD."[14] So, because we know our steps are ordered by You, help us hear You clearly. We ask in Jesus's name. Amen.

SAY THIS WITH ME

I am worth the time and attention my mind, spirit, and body require to relieve the stress and anxiety I experience every day. The Lord cares about my journey, and He will guide me and give me strength.

TRY THIS

....

Take a moment to consider your daily and weekly schedule. What is one practical step you can take this week to increase your peace? Spend a few minutes making a strategy to implement your next step.

10

Walking in Circles

··

HOW TO STOP THE WORRY WHEEL AND WALK STRAIGHT

I'm sure we've all seen it . . . the familiar scene in a movie or television show where one character says to the other, "We've been walking in circles for hours!" or "Didn't we just pass this tree?" Media plays out the all-too-real truth that when we don't have a guide leading us straight forward, we are prone to circle.

Mark Twain wrote about one such moment in his book *Roughing It*. Several men on a journey set out for Carson City in a snowstorm. One man named Ollendorff promised he could make a straight line for the city, boasting that his internal compass would lead them true. After a while, the men came across some tracks in the snow. Ollendorff used these tracks to prove his point, declaring, "Here we are, right in somebody's tracks that will hunt the way for us without any trouble. Let's hurry up and join company with the party." They picked up speed and for two hours chased after the group in front of them. What they couldn't understand was how the group's number seemed to have increased so drastically from the first few sets of tracks they saw as they set out. That's when they realized they were following their own tracks, caught in their own circle for hours and chasing no one but themselves.[1]

A scientific phenomenon is at work in this story. Scientists have found that when we lack surrounding markers to help us course correct, it is nearly impossible to walk in a straight line. This doesn't happen just when people are lost in the woods. When blindfolded, people tend to walk in some form of a circle as well. This behavior occurs with such frequency that studies have attempted to determine why we do this.[2]

Do you want to know what one group of researchers discovered? According to an article on livescience.com, "The researchers believe that loopy paths follow from a walker's changing sense of 'straight ahead.' With every step, a small deviation is likely added to a person's cognitive sense of what's straight, and these deviations accumulate to send that individual veering around in ever tighter circles as time goes on."[3]

When I think about this behavior, I cannot help but see some deep spiritual truth in it. So often, fear acts like a blindfold, keeping us from seeing what is real or what is true. It disorients us, causing us to veer from peace. Without the ability to self-correct, our thoughts create a natural bent that loops us in circles again and again and we become prisoners to the carousel of consuming worry. This is the secret of the forest of fear. Many of us become trapped in circular thinking and behaviors, going around and around the same issues in our minds, which keeps us from ever fully reaching the clearing.

The good news for us is that we have been given a compass, a guide, a tool that points to true north. While each step we take in fear might send us slightly away from peace, the Word of God is like a light, illuminating our path forward. Psalm 119:105 says, "Your word is a lamp to my feet and a light to my path."[4]

THE WORD CREATES MARKERS THAT GUIDE US STRAIGHT FORWARD.

This is why reading the Word is important. This is why the church tells us again and again to consult what God says in His Word and listen to what He has already revealed to our hearts as true so that we can easily identify when fear is trying to disorient us. The Word creates markers that guide us straight forward.

We've discussed the practical, everyday steps we can take to overcome the physical effects of anxiety in our bodies, but we need to make sure we are taking the right spiritual steps as well. Remember, the church's method of prayer and reading the Word isn't wrong. It's actually vital for our healing journey. We must make sure we are not ignoring the spiritual practices that reduce the power of fear in our lives.

So many in this world are consumed by their worries, forever following their own tracks, but we have been given a new path to follow. We have been given God's Word as our lamp, and we have been given the Holy Spirit as our guide to lead us in both spirit and truth. So, how do we keep fear from blinding us, and how do we use the Word of God as a weapon against the dark? We can take three practical spiritual steps to stop walking in circles, consumed by the same thoughts, and start making progress forward:

1. Identify what is triggering our fears, making note of our intrusive thoughts and constant worries.
2. Identify the lies we are believing, asking ourselves if what we are thinking lines up with Scripture.
3. Replace the fears and the lies with scriptural truth.

Triggered

. . . .

I have a list of fears that replays over and over in my heart, and I bet you do too. If we were to compare our lists, I'm sure they would be slightly different. Maybe you have a daughter in college and you worry about whom she is with and whether she's safe coming and going on campus. Maybe you have a son in middle school and you worry about what he has been exposed to outside your home. Maybe you have small children and you worry about what's taking place at their day care or at home with a sitter. While these all seem like widely different concerns, they are all rooted in the same fear. We are worried that something is going to happen to our children when they are away from us.

Here are some common fears many of us experience:

+ I'm afraid it's never going to get any easier.
+ I'm afraid I'm going to ruin my kids.
+ I'm afraid my own inadequacies are going to cause my children emotional pain.
+ I'm afraid God doesn't care about my journey.
+ I'm afraid I'm all alone.
+ I'm afraid I'm going to make the wrong choice.
+ I'm afraid something will happen to my kids.
+ I'm afraid I won't have enough.
+ I'm afraid I'm not truly lovable.
+ I'm afraid of rejection.
+ I'm afraid others will see through me.
+ I'm afraid I'll be judged by other moms.
+ I'm afraid I won't be enough and the ones I love will suffer in some way because I couldn't do it all.
+ I'm afraid it's too late for my kids, my spouse, or God to forgive me.

Do you identify with any of these? Often fears change our behavior. For example, maybe you're afraid you're going to make the wrong choice, so you stress over even the simplest decisions. Whereas other moms seem to know exactly what to do, perhaps you play out all the possible outcomes, unable to find one that ends well. So, you become anxious. You become anxious about the decision-making process in general. It just seems too hard! Not because a right or wrong answer exists but because you are placing so much weight on the outcome of your decision. See how that fear changes how you treat an everyday situation?

Or maybe you're afraid something will happen to your

children when you're not around, so you don't let them go anywhere without you. You make sure they are never out of your sight. The anxiety you feel is triggered when you feel as though you won't be there to protect your kids, so any suggestion from another mom to take them to the park or pick them up from school sends you into a tailspin. Maybe you say no to letting them play organized sports or ride in the car with a friend or hang out anywhere but your home.

> # WHEN OUR FEARS FEEL SO NORMAL AND THE BEHAVIORS WE DEVELOP AS A RESULT OF THEM BECOME PART OF OUR ROUTINE, IT'S HARD TO REMEMBER WHY WE ARE AFRAID.

These are just some examples of how commonly rooted fears can play out in our lives. When our fears feel so normal and the behaviors we develop as a result of them become part of our routine, it's hard to remember why we are afraid. It's not as easy to see what is causing our stress because we don't have a break from it. Sound familiar?

I want to take just a moment to pause together. If you feel anxious most of the time, do you truly know what triggers your anxiety? Do you know what is at the root of your fear? Stop right now and pray. Ask the Lord to show you what ignites that fight-or-flight response within you.

Father, when my worry seems relentless, help me remember

that You know exactly what I'm afraid of. You know when my fear started. You know what causes it. You know how it affects my daily life. Help me recognize the root of my fear. Help me identify my trigger areas. Bring to my attention the places where my heart truly needs healing, and then please help. I ask in Jesus's name. Amen.

Once you see what is triggering your fear, you can begin to overcome it. Chances are the fear you feel is rooted in some lie.

Is It True?

....

Do you remember that scene in *Peter Pan* where Peter loses his shadow? He chases it all over the nursery, toppling over nightstands and lamps, leaving a trail of chaos as the shadow repeatedly escapes and teases him. In case you missed that movie or don't remember that particular scene, eventually Peter corners his shadow and grabs it, and Wendy sews it to his shoes. Once reattached, Peter's shadow no longer seems to have a mind of its own. It waves when he waves. It moves where he moves. His shadow submits, no longer taunting him.

As a child, I watched the cartoon version of *Peter Pan* and was mostly confused. The scene was pretty funny to me. *Wait a minute,* I thought. *Shadows aren't their own things. They don't have minds or thoughts or feelings. They can't act on their own. They can't nag or torment. How silly for Peter to lose his shadow. How silly when it's just the shape on the wall behind him made by the light being blocked. How silly for Peter to have to chase it down and sew it back to his slippered shoes. That's not real.*

As an adult, I watch this scene and find myself empathizing with Peter. I understand how it feels to have shadows convince you that they are real. I understand how it feels to chase down thoughts that aren't true. And I understand how fear can seem to have a mind of its own until it is captured and told to submit.

The truth is, the Enemy uses our fears to distract us, hoping our hearts will spend time chasing shadows rather than following peace. He is terrified that we are going to recognize the power of God inside us and live it out. So he whispers lies in our ears, and each one is an assault on the character of God. Every fear we embrace is rooted in a lie that we have chosen to believe about God, His relationship to us, or who we are in Him. This goes all the way back to . . . you guessed it . . . the garden and the way Satan lied to Eve. He told her, "You will not certainly die . . . for God knows that when you eat from [the tree in the middle of the garden] your eyes will be opened, and you will be like God, knowing good and evil."[5] God had already made Eve like Himself. She didn't need to eat the fruit to become like Him. She simply needed to continue following His commands. But the lie Satan whispered was an assault against God's character as a loving creator who had already made her in His image.

EVERY FEAR SAYS, <u>GOD ISN'T WHO HE SAYS HE IS.</u>

Let's think about this for just a second. The fear that we are going to run out of something we need is an assault against God our provider. The fear that we are going to face harm is an assault against God our protector. The fear that we are alone and unseen is an assault against our God who sees! Every fear says, *God isn't who He says He is.*

It is important to identify what is triggering our fears so that we can recognize the lies we have been believing and then overcome them with truth. So, let's use the common fears I listed just a bit ago.

I'm afraid it's never going to get any easier.
Lie: It will always be just like this because God doesn't care to help me.

I'm afraid I'm going to ruin my kids.
Lie: It's up to me to raise my children in my own limited strength because God isn't guiding me.

I'm afraid my own inadequacies are going to cause my children emotional pain.
Lie: I am too broken to be a good mom, and God didn't know what He was doing when He gave me these kids.

I'm afraid God doesn't care about my journey.
Lie: God doesn't care about my journey because He is not invested in my life.

I'm afraid I'm all alone.
Lie: God is not with me.

I'm afraid I'm going to make the wrong choice.
Lie: God is not guiding me and is not powerful enough to fix my missteps.

I'm afraid something will happen to my kids.
Lie: God is not going to protect my children because He is not a protector.

I'm afraid I won't have enough.
Lie: God is not going to provide.

I'm afraid I'm not truly lovable.
Lie: My worth is dependent on my performance, not on God's perfect love.

I'm afraid of rejection.
Lie: I'm not good enough.

I'm afraid others will see through me.
Lie: I should be ashamed of who I really am.

I'm afraid I'll be judged by other moms.
Lie: My identity is found in the approval of others.

I'm afraid I won't be enough and the ones I love will suffer in some way because I couldn't do it all.
Lie: God's strength is not made perfect in my weakness.

I'm afraid it's too late for my kids, my spouse, or God to forgive me.
Lie: I'm not worthy of forgiveness.

Do you see how each fear reveals some lie we've been believing? Sis, don't feel ashamed. I'm not pointing this out to condemn you. I'm pointing out these lies to free you from their power. When we pull lies from the shadows, we immediately begin to disarm them. But I know how you might be feeling this minute. In this exact moment, as these lies have been exposed, the Enemy wants to trap you. He wants you to feel so embarrassed about believing these lies that you sit down, stop journeying toward peace, and ask, *What's wrong with me? How could I believe this way? Is something wrong with my faith?* It's the same gross tactic the Enemy uses to tell us we should be ashamed for being broken so that we don't get the help we need and instead sit alone in our suffering.

Don't give him any room! Shake off those feelings of guilt right now. Scripture says, "There is now no condemnation for those who are in Christ Jesus."[6] Remember, the Holy Spirit helps illuminate areas of struggle in our lives. The Holy Spirit says, *You have a problem. Let's fix it!* whereas the Enemy says, *You are the problem. You're worthless.* The Holy Spirit convicts our hearts to free us, and the Enemy condemns us to bind us. If you've been believing lies like the ones I listed, know that God wants to set your heart completely free right now. He wants to use this exposure of these previously hidden deceptions to take your journey toward peace even further. You prayed and asked the Lord to show you what triggers your fear. Now pray and ask the Lord to show you what nontruths you've been believing.

Father, thank You for not condemning me. Thank You, God,

*for the beautiful exchange of the fear in my heart for Your perfect
peace. Thank You for setting my heart completely free. Help me
identify the lies I have been believing so I can exchange them for
Your truth. I ask in Jesus's name. Amen.*

Once we see the lies, we can grab them (as Peter Pan did
with his shadow) and tell them they aren't real, they don't
have any power over us, they can't taunt us, and they have to
bow to the truth of who God says He is in His Word.

Let's look at the process of exchanging fear for what God
says is true.

Anchor into Truth

In Paul's letter to the Philippians, he said, "Don't worry
about anything; instead, pray about everything. Tell God
what you need, and thank him for all he has done. Then you
will experience God's peace, which exceeds anything we can
understand. His peace will guard your hearts and minds as
you live in Christ Jesus."[7]

First, he told them to pray. Second, to tell God what they
need. Third, to thank God for what He has done. But then
Paul went on to give them an important final step. He said,
"And now, dear brothers and sisters, one final thing. Fix your
thoughts on what is true, and honorable, and right, and pure,
and lovely, and admirable. Think about things that are excellent and worthy of praise."[8]

The next step in walking toward peace is fixing our

thoughts on what is good and pure. It's great to identify our fears. It's even more powerful to recognize the lies that feed the roots of those fears. But if we are going to complete this process, we have to take Paul's advice. We must replace the lies we've been believing with God's truth.

How do we practically live out this process? How do we strategically capture those fears and replace them with what God says is true? Scripture gives us a plan. See, Paul pointed out what we should be thinking about—things that are true, honorable, right, pure, lovely, admirable, excellent, and worthy of praise. (Notice that doom, gloom, and kaboom are not on that list.) So, when our minds want to bend toward fear and when the natural direction of our steps deviates us little bit by little bit away from what is true, how do we walk straight? We do two things to keep our minds following what Paul suggested: we go to the Word of God to remind ourselves of what God has already said is true, and we consult the Holy Spirit.

In God's Word, He reveals clearly His character. He reveals that He is kind, compassionate, and slow to anger. He reveals that He is ever present, loving, and protecting. He reveals that He has overcome the world, put an end to the power of sin and death, and removed the power of condemnation. If we struggle with anxiety, reading our Bibles and reminding ourselves again and again of God's character is paramount to dismantling the darkness. But we haven't been given only His Word.

In addition to God's Word, 1 Corinthians 2:16 says, "We have the mind of Christ." So, we have the Bible, and we have the Spirit of God Himself. We always have access to God's leading, teaching, and course correcting. Even when our minds want to race or run away or lead us down paths that aren't true, we have access to God's thoughts, and we can ask Him to trade our thoughts for His.

What do I mean we have access to God's thoughts? I know it sounds sort of mystical. Scripture makes it really clear, however. Remember, the Word says, "Who knows a person's thoughts except their own spirit within them? In the same way no one knows the thoughts of God except the Spirit of God. What we have received is not the spirit of the world, but the Spirit who is from God, so that we may understand what God has freely given us."[9] Break it down. We have been given the Spirit of God, and the Spirit of God knows His own thoughts. Simple.

So, we take captive every thought that doesn't line up with what God says is true about Himself. Paul said in 2 Corinthians 10:3–5, "Though we walk in the flesh, we do not war according to the flesh. For the weapons of our warfare are not carnal but mighty in God for pulling down strongholds, casting down arguments and every high thing that exalts itself against the knowledge of God, bringing every thought into captivity to the obedience of Christ."[10]

Basically, we train ourselves to say, *No, thought! You don't get to exalt yourself higher than what God says is true. You have to obey Christ.* We recognize the lie as quickly as we think it, and we don't give it any room to grow into fear in our hearts.

Here's our practical lie-replacement strategy, step by step, including what we have read in previous chapters.

Step 1: Feel afraid/triggered.

Step 2: Pause to remember that our bodies are releasing chemicals to make us feel a rush of hormones.

Step 3: Pray, ask God to give us supernatural joy, and begin laughing at the Enemy's plan so we can combat those hormones and the physical responses of our bodies toward the fear.

Step 4: Identify the lie at the root of our fear. Ask, *What does this fear say about who God is? Is it true?*

Step 5: Take the thought captive, refusing to follow it into the dark. Ask God to reveal His truth through His Word and by the power of the Holy Spirit.

Step 6: Repeat steps 2 through 5.

MY FEARS FEEL SO MUCH BIGGER THAN I AM, BUT GOD IS EVEN BIGGER.

I love imagining what it would look like in real life to grab hold of our racing thoughts, drag them before Jesus, and make them bow to who He is. So often my fears feel so much bigger than I am, but God is even bigger. He is still on His throne. He is still victorious over it all. And He is still very much interested in helping me. So, let's look back at our list of common fears one last time, and let's place them at the feet of Jesus. Let's ask Him to give us His truth instead. Say each truth out loud as you come to it!

I'm afraid it's never going to get any easier.
Lie: It will always be just like this because God doesn't care to help me.
Truth: God cares about me, and He will help me. It won't always be this hard.

I'm afraid I'm going to ruin my kids.
Lie: It's up to me to raise my children in my own limited strength because God isn't guiding me.
Truth: God is guiding me and gives me His wisdom and strength. God is helping me raise my children.

I'm afraid my own inadequacies are going to cause my children emotional pain.
Lie: I am too broken to be a good mom, and God didn't know what He was doing when He gave me these kids.
Truth: God knew exactly what He was doing when He made me a momma to these children, because He is all knowing. I'm not too broken to be a good mom. God is helping me daily.

I'm afraid God doesn't care about my journey.
Lie: God doesn't care about my journey because He is not invested in my life.
Truth: God cares about my journey because He is intimately invested in every area of my life. He orders my steps and has a good future for me.

I'm afraid I'm all alone.
Lie: God is not with me.
Truth: God is always with me and never leaves me.

I'm afraid I'm going to make the wrong choice.
Lie: God is not guiding me and is not powerful enough to fix my missteps.
Truth: God is guiding me and gives me His wisdom freely.

I'm afraid something will happen to my kids.
Lie: God is not going to protect my children because He is not a protector.
Truth: God is our protector.

I'm afraid I won't have enough.
Lie: God is not going to provide.
Truth: God is my provider.

I'm afraid I'm not truly lovable.
Lie: My worth is dependent on my performance, not on God's perfect love.
Truth: I am loved because my worth is fully determined by God's perfect love and His sacrifice.

I'm afraid of rejection.
Lie: I'm not good enough.
Truth: I'm more than enough with Jesus!

I'm afraid others will see through me.
Lie: I should be ashamed of who I really am.
Truth: I am loved and accepted by God, and there is no condemnation for those in Christ Jesus.

I'm afraid I'll be judged by other moms.
Lie: My identity is found in the approval of others.
Truth: I have the approval of heaven, and my identity is found in being a daughter of God, bought with Jesus's blood and made in God's image.

I'm afraid I won't be enough and the ones I love will suffer in some way because I couldn't do it all.
Lie: God's strength is not made perfect in my weakness.
Truth: God's strength is made perfect in my weakness, and He is filling in all my gaps. He won't leave me to figure it all out on my own.

I'm afraid it's too late for my kids, my spouse, or God to forgive me.
Lie: I'm not worthy of forgiveness.
Truth: I'm worthy of forgiveness and mercy. I deserve a fresh start so I can move from a place of guilt to a place of grace.

Can you sense the freedom that will come from having an entire arsenal of truth to fire back at the lies of the Enemy? Can you see how strengthening your spirit and remaining rooted in truth can keep you walking straight out of the forest of fear? Do you realize how free you can be from your relentless thoughts that keep you looping in circles? Sis, I can't do anything about what's going on in your body. But I can absolutely walk you right up to Truth Himself and say,

"He has heart solutions. He can disarm fear. He can make lies bow. He can uproot shame and pain and the emotional junk you've been carrying for too long."

Your heart might race. Your chest might feel tight. You might feel physically as if the walls are closing in and you won't ever be in control again, but spiritually? In the supernatural? You're steady. You're anchored. You're secure.

In my own life, I've learned to say,

Race, heart. Just try it. Go for it. Panic away. Because these emotions I'm experiencing are how I'm feeling, but they aren't who I am. I know truth. I know what God says. I'm free. I'm powerful. I'm loved and held. I'm in a broken body, but God has already set my spirit free from this torment. So, today, I stand in victory. Victory that might not look like others expect it to but victory that is available to me because Jesus loves me and promised not to leave me alone in my suffering. I'm here in this body, but I'm also seated with Christ Jesus in heavenly places right now because what His Word tells me is true. So, while fear wants to run rampant, my spirit remains anchored right here at the feet of Jesus, and together we are going to walk steadily forward right through this darkness. I will make it out of this forest alive because I am fully held and led by the arms of Peace.

Let's Pray Together

....

Father, thank You for the spiritual strategy to overcome what would try to consume us. Help us stay anchored in who You are and what You say is true. As each fear manifests itself in our lives, help us think clearly of Your truth. Speak loudly, Lord. Give us Your thoughts and Your peace. Flood our hearts with what You say about who You are and who we are. Silence the Enemy. Take hold of every fear. You have "not given us a spirit of fear, but of power and of love and of a sound mind."[11] Remove the power of fear in our lives. We ask in Jesus's name. Amen.

Say This with Me

....

Every fear must bow to the name of Jesus. I'm overcoming fear step by step, day by day. My eyes are open to Truth, and I will follow Him straight forward.

Try This

....

Grab your journal and make a list of some of your greatest areas of anxiety. Can you identify the lies at their roots? Spend a moment writing out truth from God's Word to dismantle each lie. Use pages 177–79 for reference.

II

Lost and Found

·····················

GOING BACK INTO THE FOREST
TO WALK OTHER WOMEN TOWARD FREEDOM

ast year, Jared and I took the kids back to Oklahoma during the summer. We spent about three weeks with friends and family because no matter where you end up in life, sometimes it's just good to be back where your roots are. While there, we decided to meet up with some friends at a popular children's museum. Our friends had never been there, and my children, who could describe in detail every exhibit, were thrilled to show them around.

We weren't the only ones who had the idea to beat the blazing Oklahoma heat by taking the family to an indoor museum. The building was buzzing with activity. My friend and I looked at the crowd and decided it would be a good idea to go over some rules about what to do just in case one of our kids got separated from the group. Our guidelines were simple:

1. If you get lost, stay right where you are. We will look for you. Just stay put and remember that we are looking for you!

2. Tell someone you are lost. Don't be shy. If you are scared and it's taking us too long to get to you, tell a mommy close by.

3. Stay calm. We aren't going to leave the building without you. We aren't going to keep having fun without you. We are always checking to make sure everyone is close and safe. We will come for you. Don't panic and do *not* leave, even if a mommy tells you she can take you to an adult who can help. The adults who work there can come to you. You stay put.

Wide-eyed, the kids seemed to take in all the rules. None of them seemed too worried, but I could tell they had listened and were aware that this was a place one could easily get lost. I was glad they had paid attention. Farther into the building, I immediately knew keeping track of them would be a challenge. They all wanted to go in different directions. Many exhibits and hands-on activities were close to one another, and it would be easy for one of the five kids to wander away without even realizing he had left the group. It would take very watchful eyes to make sure everyone stayed together.

We hadn't been there even fifteen minutes, and I hadn't stopped naming all the children in our group over and over in my mind, counting each one and making note that everyone was still with us. *Kolton, Kadence, Jaxton . . . Where's Carolina? There she is. Mayah. Kolton . . . Where's Kadence? There's Kadence. Jaxton, Carolina, Mayah.* Again and again.

I was midway through a head count when I felt the little

tap. I looked down to see a little blond girl with tears in her eyes. "I can't find my mommy," she said, beginning to cry harder. The admission that she was lost broke the wall of the tears she was holding back, and she just let them flow.

I crouched down to her level to help her see me and know she wasn't alone.

"What's your name?" I asked.

"Sarah."

"Hi, Sarah. My name is Becky, and I have very good news for you. Your momma is looking for you right now. Because that's what mommas do when they can't find their little girls. I'm going to have my friend go get someone who works here, and they will help us get your momma to you. Can you tell me your mom's name or what she looks like?"

Sarah stopped crying. She wasn't any closer to her mom, but she was a lot less lost. There's something powerful about knowing you're not alone. It seems to disarm a layer of fear immediately.

Sarah began to describe her mom. Her hair. Her clothes. That's when Sarah's momma came around the corner. I smiled and said, "See! Your mommy was looking for you!" I told her mom all about how brave Sarah had been. How she did exactly what I had told my own kids to do. She was scared but found a mom and told her that she was lost, and she stayed put until her mom came for her. The momma looked down at Sarah and hugged her tightly, and they left to rejoin the rest of their family.

I think of that afternoon often. That quick interaction with Sarah taught me some important lessons on being lost, being found, and helping others who are lost become found.

On Being Lost

· · · · · · · · · · · · · · · · · · · ·

I have been lost once in my life. I was on an elementary school field trip attended by nearly the entire Oklahoma City metro area, or so it seemed. Multiple schools from many districts had sent busloads of students to the event center. I honestly can't remember anything about the program except some guy standing on stage, singing about e-e-e-erosion and explaining the importance of lakes and streams. As far as field trips go, competing with the skating rink or the zoo, it ranked pretty low on my list of favorites. That, and I completely confused the purpose of the field trip. I didn't think we were going to a presentation on erosion; for some reason I thought we were going to a laser light show. I don't remember why I thought it, but I was very confused about the field trip and kept waiting for some cool '90s tech production to begin. It never did. But a light show was about to begin just outside.

A springtime storm had moved into the area just as the program was ending, and every teacher decided to try to get her class out first. It was total chaos: ten thousand students and teachers leaving the arena at once. "Follow the classmate in front of you," my teacher shouted down our row. "Everyone, stay together." Obviously, staying together is always the goal. But on this day . . . well . . . I was near the back with just two or three kids behind me in our group of about twenty-five. The boy I was following had straight light brown hair, and I made sure that no matter what happened, he was right in front of me.

As I followed him out of the event center and into the rain, I raced through the parking lot in a long line of students, snaking my way past moving buses and toward the safety of my own. I climbed onto the bus, soaking wet, thrilled to be out of the storm ... and immediately I realized I didn't recognize one person looking back at me.

I turned around, and the boy with the brown hair followed me. About three of my classmates and I wandered back out into the very busy parking lot and started to walk ... somewhere. The storm was getting worse. We didn't know where we were going, but we knew we couldn't stay where we were. Bus after bus began to pull out, and we all felt unseen and very unsafe. That's when she showed up.

This woman carrying a wide umbrella and wearing a white wind suit (Yes, '90s fashion!) came out of nowhere and asked if we were lost. I burst into tears and said "Yes!" as if we would never be found, as if our teacher would leave the event center and drive all the way back to school before realizing we were sitting on the curb in the thunderstorm.

"Can you help us?"

I remember her answer very clearly.

"Yes! I know where your teacher is. Let's go this way!"

I didn't think about her answer until later that night when I was tucked safely into my bed. *I know where your teacher is.* She took us under her umbrella and walked us straight to our bus. As the doors opened and everyone began to climb inside, I remember turning around to thank the woman, but she was gone. I looked up and down the row of buses and out across the parking lot, but the kind woman in the white wind suit had vanished.

To this day, I think about how she didn't ask us our names, we didn't have any identifying school shirts on, and she never asked who our teacher was or what school we went to. She just looked at us, told us she knew where our teacher was, and took us right to her.

As I was falling asleep that night, I remember my momma saying, "I'm so glad that angel came to help you." And I was too. I was so glad.

Something happens when we become lost. Fear rises, and we believe every lie easily. We believe that we will never be found. We believe that no one sees us. We sense danger, and we panic quickly. But Sarah at the children's museum and I as a child had something in common: the realization that we were not alone lifted the power of fear.

LET THE TRUTH THAT YOU ARE SEEN SETTLE DEEPLY INTO YOUR HEART.

I hope as you have been reading, you have let the truth that you are seen settle deeply into your heart. You have the Holy Spirit with you, and you also have me. You have the realization that you aren't wandering on your own anymore. You're not the only woman deep in the throes of trying to find your way forward through the fear. But you still might need to do something. You might need to tell someone in your life exactly where you are. You might need to tell someone near you, "I feel lost."

The *Los Angeles Times* recently published an article outlining steps to ensure people are found should they suddenly become lost while hiking.[1] One of those steps is to call for help and be able to describe where they are to their rescuers, using language such as "I'm east of the tree line" or "I'm west of the river." The experts explained that it helps rescuers find hikers faster if they can accurately describe where they are.

So, I want to ask you, friend, Where are you? What is daily anxiety like for you? Are you deep in struggles that cripple your ability to think straight? Could you describe what you're feeling to rescuers? Could you put language to what you feel and think? If you have lost your peace, the first thing you should do is tell someone so she can help you find it.

At the beginning, we talked about the shame so many Christian women feel about the anxiety they live with. Friend, we don't have time to waste when we are out here in the woods. We don't have time to sit down and give up and just pretend we are okay. We've talked too much about how common anxiety is to believe for one more second the lie that we should keep silent rather than shout for help. This is where you scream, sis. This is where you call out to those you trust, those who can help, those who will walk with you out of here. This is where you cry, "I've lost my peace, and I need help finding my way back to joy." And you let the rescuers come. Look around. Are you where you want to be?

On Being Found

....

I cannot describe the feeling of relief I experienced when that lady with her giant umbrella said she knew the way to my teacher. I'm sure it was similar to what Sarah felt when I told her I'd stay with her until her momma came. It's one thing to know you're not alone. But you experience a whole new level of comfort when someone tells you she will stay with you until you are where you want to be. And it's even more empowering to be with someone who knows what you need to do next to get to where you want to be.

Because being found doesn't mean you're out of the woods; it just means someone can lead you out of the woods. Right? When you're hiking in the forest, the moment you're no longer lost is when the rescuer comes, not when you leave the forest.

BEING FOUND ISN'T THE ABSENCE OF THE FOREST. IT IS THE PRESENCE OF A GUIDE!

Let's think about what this means for you in this forest of fear. The moment you say you need help and your friend, family member, pastor, or another professional joins you on your journey, you aren't lost anymore. You might not be where you want to be yet, but you aren't wandering alone without direction. What a powerful thought! Being found isn't the absence of the forest. It is the presence of a guide! Come on! That will preach.

This is why we must be adamant about letting people join us as we journey. This is why we cannot think for even a second that we should try to walk this path alone. The Holy Spirit wants to guide us, and He does. He is our ultimate guide. But we need people to hold us up, encourage us, and lead us to where we ultimately want to be.

My prayer as I have written this book is that you would feel found. I have prayed that through these words, you would realize you aren't alone. But we must do something together now. Once we are found, we must learn how to help others who are lost be found as well.

On Helping Those Who Are Lost Be Found

You and I are not the only women we know who find ourselves in these woods of worry. We aren't the only ones who need to face racing imaginations, scavenging raccoons, intimidating wolves, and the danger of walking in circles. We aren't the only ones who are told, "Pray more! Worry less! Your faith is faulty!" We aren't the only women who stay silent rather than shout for help. We aren't the only Christian women with anxiety.

Other women are out here with us, and as we find our way to the clearing, where the dark forest doesn't seem so overwhelming anymore, where we realize that even in the midst of the darkness we can have peace because God is with us, we need to be ready to take our next steps. We need to check the batteries in our flashlights, find some good hiking boots, grab some gear, and head back into the forest to rescue as many other women as we can. You with me?

Jesus said specifically that He "came to seek and to save the lost."[2] Finding those who were alone or had been forgotten in some way was a key theme of Jesus's earthly ministry. He shared a story about a lost sheep, a lost coin, and a lost son.[3] Searching for the one who has gone astray is a principle of the kingdom of heaven.

Think of the story Jesus told in Luke 15:4–6 about the lost sheep: "Suppose one of you has a hundred sheep and loses one of them. Doesn't he leave the ninety-nine in the open country and go after the lost sheep until he finds it? And when he finds it, he joyfully puts it on his shoulders and goes home. Then he calls his friends and neighbors together and says, 'Rejoice with me; I have found my lost sheep.'"

Jesus was talking about those who are separated from Him spiritually and have yet to be saved by His grace, but a core value of the kingdom of God is on display in this passage. Jesus made it clear that it is our mission as those who have been found to help find those who are lost.

So, how do we practically go back into the forest for our sisters who are struggling with anxiety? We become really good trail guides, friend.

Becoming a Trail Guide

....

I have to ask: On your journey through the forest of anxiety, did you plan on ever having to lead someone else out? I didn't. I suppose that's kind of strange to admit now, but in the initial stages of writing this book, I sat in a coffee shop parking lot, called my momma, and cried, "What business do I have leading other women when I feel just as lost as they do? Who am I to think of myself as some sort of leader in this area? I know what it feels like to live with anxiety. I know what it feels like to work through it each day. But I'm not whole. I'm not cured. I'm found, but I'm still in the forest!"

THE FEAR I FEEL DOESN'T DEFINE MY FAITH BECAUSE I AM NOT MY EMOTIONS.

My own words have bounced back at me a few times in life. These words bounced back with some force: *Found but still in the forest.* I think that's where so many of us who struggle with chronic anxiety are most of the time. Yet because we spend time in the forest, we disqualify ourselves from leading or teaching or thinking of ourselves as powerful women full of faith. But I'm done with it. The fear I feel doesn't define my faith because I am not my emotions.

I said it at the beginning. I'll say it here at the end. I have anxiety. I am a Christian woman full of faith. They are independent facts about me. While I'm panicking, wanting to hide and avoid everything that must be done, and while I'm trying to intentionally calm my breathing or stop my racing thoughts, the Holy Spirit is with me. He's reminding me that I am not my emotions. I am not my nutritional deficiencies. I'm not my diagnosis or my broken DNA.

I am a loved daughter. A cherished wife. An amazing mom. A good friend. And a powerful voice for hope in the midst of all seasons and situations. I am seen. I am held. And I'm found in the eyes of those who love me and the One who lives in me. And so are you.

That's the powerful promise of peace. Jesus walks across relentless waves. He stands amid strong winds. We focus on the part where He calms the winds and waves by declaring they must obey . . . and they do. But peace is present and remains steady even amid the madness. That peace is in us. He is steady even when storms are raging around us or within us. He's with us both even now, friend. *Even now.*

NO ONE IS MORE SKILLED IN BEING A TRAIL GUIDE THAN SOMEONE WHO KNOWS THE PATH WELL.

That's what qualifies me to lead other women with anxiety, and that's what qualifies you to do the same. No one is more skilled in being a trail guide than someone who knows the path well. And that is us. We know these woods.

That means we aren't going to leave our sisters behind. We aren't going to feel found ourselves and not go back in for others. So, what's the first step in going back into the forest? We must remember that the people we are going back in for are weary and might not be calling for help, so we have to be loud.

I read a story once about a hiker who had gone off course while on a short lunch-break hike. He became disoriented, ran out of energy, and was just plain lost and exhausted. A volunteer searcher found him. Often when people go missing, search and rescue (SAR) teams are aided by volunteers. Even though in this story, the search and rescue team didn't want this nontrained volunteer to join the search, he said he felt as though he needed to. He followed a path and, because he was a skilled climber, began to climb. As he climbed, he called out for the lost man. The man was able to muster enough energy to call back, and he was ultimately found. That's why SAR teams often wear whistles and recommend that hikers wear them too. Sometimes it just takes too much physical effort to yell for help.

What does this have to do with us? The women who need to know what you know might not be calling for help. They might be hiding in shame or embarrassment. They might be too exhausted or feel too helpless to call out into the darkness. They might be trying to conceal their anxiety, manage it on their own, or even ignore it. If you're going to be part of the search and rescue team that helps other women be found, then you might have to blow your whistle so they can call back to you for help. That looks like sharing your story with the mom who says she's worried. It looks like being open and honest about your struggles with your moms' group or your friends. It looks like disarming the lie that says women with anxiety are too broken to lead. You blaze a trail for these women, friend. You blaze a trail with your courage to share your story, and you create a place for them to join your journey. You call out to them so they can call back to you. You blow the whistle first.

Prepare for Future Hikers

If you are going to lead a group of women, it is important for you to know two things. First, you need to know the steps you're going to take. Second, you need to know where you are going. This is true no matter the circumstances surrounding your leadership. A leader without a direction is dangerous. As you prepare to find women who are struggling and lead them out of this forest of fear, you need to know the trail. You need to be able to show those you're guiding how to climb over obstacles and how to navigate uncomfortable situations. That means you need to be taking notes as you walk.

Experts who train hikers tell them to turn their heads around every now and then so they know what the trail looks like in the other direction. A hiker knows what it looks like going forward, but what does it look like to someone going the other way? A trail leader needs to be familiar with a 360-degree perspective of the path. Professionals suggest that hikers make mental notes or even take photographs of where they have been if they plan on leading others on the trail at some point.

How do you do this when it comes to anxiety? As you experience moments of anxiety, take a minute to look at it from all angles. Document it. Write about your experiences in a journal. Write about how God met you. Grab your phone and record your thoughts and feelings. Record what you're experiencing as you journey. Ask yourself, *What does this look like from the outside looking in?* You might need to share with another mom how you got through it.

A few days ago, I stood in my kitchen, panicking. I wasn't having a panic attack. I was able to catch my breath. I could think clearly. My body wasn't out of control. I just felt fully overwhelmed and anxious. Do you know what I did? I told my husband. "Remind me that it's not always going to be this hard," I said. "Remind me that this feeling will pass." So he did, and it did.

But in that moment, I did something I don't usually do. I sort of stepped outside the situation and looked at it as an outsider. I asked myself, *What would I tell someone going through this exact experience?* I made a note of what I would say, and do you know what happened? Two days later, my momma called me to tell me how she was feeling. Do you know what I told her? I used the mental notes I had made just a few days before to walk her through that moment.

That's what it looks like to be involved in search and rescue. You look around and realize that at some point, you might be back at this place and you might need to know what direction to go. You might have these emotions again. You might feel these fears. You might think these thoughts.

Or someone you know might be in this place at some point too. So, you mark the trail and take notes on your map and say to yourself, *If I ever find myself in this place again, this is how I get out of it.* Are you documenting your journey well enough that you could use it as a resource to help yourself or another momma?

Finally, as someone prepared to go back in and free other women from the power of fear in their lives, you must remember where you're leading them—to Jesus. He's the goal. He knows the full course ahead. He's the one who will help you remember all the training we have talked about in these eleven chapters.

He will help you remember the importance of dismantling your fear of the dark. He's the one who leads you on a personalized path to peace. He will tell you that the fears you face seem big but that He is bigger. He will remind you that the Holy Spirit is within you. He will remind you that trail angels are important and that we were never meant to journey alone. He will help you recapture your imagination because the only future that exists is one where He promises to meet you. He will help you fight the wolves and face what makes you anxious. He will help you destroy scavengers. He will lead you as you take practical steps toward peace in whatever ways help you most. And He will keep you from walking in circles as your mind stays focused ahead on what is true.

He is leading you as you prepare to lead others. You are ready. You know what to do and what to say to help other women find freedom. And, friend, even now women are waiting to be found and will be rescued because of your brave decision to go back in and help them.

At the beginning, I said I couldn't promise that you would reach the clearing by the end of our time together. I couldn't guarantee that you would be free from fear. But I did promise that we would encounter Peace Himself, who takes the power of fear and walks us through every dark night. And we have. We are found in Him. He is with you, leading you steadily on. He is wrapping you in His love. And He is ready to use you to dismantle the darkness and connect other mommas to His hope. All He needs is your yes. I have a feeling, this wonderful feeling, that you are clicking on your flashlight and whispering your yes even now.

"Helloooo?" they cry into the dark night.

"We're coming!" we call from the other side.

LET'S PRAY TOGETHER

Father, thank You for the gift of lives spent following You. Thank You for using us, despite our brokenness, to help others find healing and freedom. We love You. We love who You have revealed Yourself to be, even in our suffering, God. You have shown Yourself to be a God of compassion. You're a God of mercy. You're a God who heals. You're a God who doesn't cause our pain or grief but uses it for good. Use our lives, God, as living sacrifices. May we always point to the hope found in Your sacrifice.

Help us remember the truths found in Your Word. Help us remember who You really are, and help us remember who we are in You. We are found in You. We are loved by You. We are held and led by You. Send us in to find our sisters who need the same freedom we have found from the lies we used to believe. Send us in to rescue others from darkness. You came to save that which was lost. Allow us the privilege of joining You in Your kingdom mission. Continue to heal us, God—mentally, physically, spiritually, and emotionally. Supernaturally free us from the power of fear in our lives even now. And lead us steadily on in Your love. We ask in Jesus's name. Amen.

SAY THIS WITH ME

I am equipped to help other women who struggle with anxiety find help, hope, and healing. I say, *Yes, Lord. Use my life to find those who are lost so You can free them from fear.*

TRY THIS

Make a list of the women in your life who are also walking through anxiety. Pray for them. What is one way that you can "go back into the forest" for these women this week? What have you learned that you want them to know as well?

Before You Go

·······················

In early 2020, the world changed. What once felt sure became uncertain. What was previously solid ground shifted beneath our feet. Sickness spread. Isolation became mandatory. The unknowns grew. And a new wave of fear slipped into homes across the globe.

We all traveled collectively through the dark time, remembering that while distance meant we couldn't reach out and hold on to one another, we were not alone in what we were feeling or experiencing.

Late one night as I sheltered in place, I sat awake in bed, wondering and worrying, all while doing my best to worship Jesus instead. I prayed. I poured out my heart to Him. And we had a simple yet important conversation that I'd like to share with you:

ME: Okay, God, here's the thing. I'm scared. I'm trying not to be, but I am.

GOD: I know. Want to talk about it?

ME: Do we need to? I mean, You already know.

GOD: Let's talk about it anyway . . . We've done this before.

ME: I know. I just feel like I should be bigger or stronger or something by now.

GOD: *waits patiently, unhurried, undistracted, never annoyed*

ME: I'm afraid I'll do everything I can to protect my family and it won't be enough. I'm afraid of someone I love dying. I'm afraid the world won't go back to what it was before. I'm afraid my life is always going to feel a little bit unsettled.

GOD: Anything else?

ME: Everything else.

GOD: Remember how Jaxton woke up the other night and came running down the hall to your bedroom?

ME: Yes.

GOD: You were still awake, so when you heard him running, you started calling out to him before he even got to you. Remember? Do you remember what you called out to him?

ME: I said, "You're okay! You're okay! You're okay!"

GOD: Why did you call to him? Why didn't you just wait for him to get to your room?

ME: Because I wanted him to know before he reached the end of the dark hallway that I was awake and had heard him and that he didn't have to be afraid.

GOD: Exactly. I hear you, daughter. I hear your thoughts racing like feet down the dark hallway. There's another side to all of this. I'm there already. I've seen the end of it. And I want you to know, right here as you walk through it all, that you're okay. I haven't gone to sleep, and I won't.

ME: *crying* Can we sit together for a while? Can we just sit here a minute before I go back to facing it all?

GOD: There's nothing I'd love more.

Peace came in that moment. Not peace from answered questions or a threat that had suddenly passed. Peace, in the form of God Himself, came close and met me right there in the dark. He is the same Peace who will meet you again and again.

Before you go, I want to remind you that no matter what lies ahead, no matter what is just over the horizon or beyond your view, the Lord has already seen it, has prepared for it, and will walk you through it. So, even when the world feels big and we sometimes feel small and when we don't know what tomorrow holds, we reach out our hands, take hold of His, and listen as He speaks over us the promise of John 14:27:

Peace I leave with you; my peace I give you. I do not give to you as the world gives. Do not let your hearts be troubled and do not be afraid.

Notes

· · · · · · · · · ·

To You, Momma, Before We Begin

1. Philippians 4:6, NKJV.

1: Unafraid of the Dark

1. "What Are Anxiety Disorders?," American Psychiatric Association, January 2017, www.psychiatry.org/patients-families /anxiety-disorders/what-are-anxiety-disorders.
2. "What Are Anxiety Disorders?"
3. "What Are Anxiety Disorders?"
4. *Encyclopaedia Britannica Online*, s.v. "autonomic nervous system," www.britannica.com/science/autonomic -nervous-system.
5. *Britannica Online*, "autonomic nervous system."
6. Paul Meier, "How to Understand Major Mental Health Disorders," in *The Struggle Is Real: How to Care for Mental and Relational Health Needs in the Church*, ed. Dr. Tim Clinton and Dr. Jared Pingleton (Bloomington, IN: WestBow, 2019), 27.

2: Personalized Pathways to Peace

1. "Facts and Statistics," Anxiety and Depression Association of America, https://adaa.org/about-adaa/press-room/facts -statistics.

2. Matthew 20:32.

3. John 9:3.

4. John 9:7.

5. John 2:3.

6. John 2:11.

7. See Matthew 14:13–21; 15:29–39.

8. See Matthew 8:23–27; Mark 4:35–41; Luke 8:22–25.

9. See John 11:1–44.

10. Numbers 14:2, NLT.

11. See Lamentations 3:22–23, NKJV.

3: Lions, Tigers, and a Million Modern Fears (Oh My!)

1. "Anxiety During Pregnancy and Postpartum," Postpartum Support International, www.postpartum.net/learn-more /anxiety-during-pregnancy-postpartum.

2. Ecclesiastes 4:10, NLT.

3. Jamie Ballard, "25 Funny Parenting Quotes That Will Have You Saying 'So True,'" *Good Housekeeping*, July 20, 2018, www.goodhousekeeping.com/life/parenting/g4931/funny -parenting-quotes/?slide=15.

4. Sarah Schreiber, "Hero Mom Miraculously Held Onto Her Baby as a Tornado Tossed Them in the Air," *Good Housekeeping*, February 9, 2017, www.goodhousekeeping.com/life /parenting/news/a42816/mom-tornado-saves-daughter-car -seat.

5. Psalm 91, NLT.

4: Holy Spirit Wilderness Guide

1. Genesis 1:28.

2. Romans 7:15.

3. Romans 8:5.

4. Romans 8:9–11.

5. John 14:15–17 (emphasis mine).

6. *Strong's Concordance,* s.v. "paraklétos," 3875, Bible Hub, https://biblehub.com/greek/3875.htm.

7. HELPS Word-studies, s.v. "allos," 243, Bible Hub, https://biblehub.com/greek/243.htm.

8. 1 Corinthians 2:10–12, NLT.

9. John 16:7, NLT.

5: TRAIL ANGELS

1. Proverbs 28:1, NLT.

2. Galatians 6:2.

3. Markham Heid, "The Loneliness Epidemic," *Time Special Edition: Mental Health: A New Understanding,* 2018, 16–18.

4. Genesis 2:18, NKJV.

5. Ceylan Yeginsu, "U.K. Appoints a Minister for Loneliness," *New York Times,* January 17, 2018, www.nytimes.com/2018/01/17/world/europe/uk-britain-loneliness.html.

6. Luke 5:17–26, NLT.

7. 1 Peter 5:7, NKJV.

6: FIRE IN THE FOREST

1. Genesis 1:26–27, NLT.

2. Genesis 2:7, NLT.

3. Deuteronomy 8:7–10.

4. Deuteronomy 8:18–20, NLT.

5. Ezra 1:2–4.

6. 1 Corinthians 2:9, NLT.

7: FACE THE WOLF

1. Dina Spector, "What to Do If You Are Attacked by a Pack of Wolves," Business Insider, June 28, 2012, www.business insider.com/what-to-do-if-you-are-attacked-by-a-pack-of -wolves-2012-6.
2. 1 John 4:4, NKJV.

8: RACCOONS AND OTHER SCAVENGERS

1. "About the Caffeine Molecule—Chemical and Physical Properties," Science of Cooking, www.scienceofcooking .com/caffeine.htm.
2. Anthea Levi, "Why Drinking Coffee Might Be Fueling Your Anxiety," *Health*, December 10, 2018, www.health.com /anxiety/how-coffee-increases-anxiety.
3. Francis M. Torres, "Caffeine-Induced Psychiatric Disorders," *Pulse*, April 2009, www.americanmedtech.org/files/STEP _Online_articles/353.pdf.
4. "Why Electronics May Stimulate You Before Bed," National Sleep Foundation, www.sleepfoundation.org/articles/why -electronics-may-stimulate-you-bed.
5. "Electronics May Stimulate You."
6. See Colossians 3:15, NKJV.

9: SENSIBLE STEPPING-STONES

1. Joseph Rauch, "Different Types of Anxiety Disorders: How Are They Classified?," Talkspace, May 23, 2017, www.talk space.com/blog/different-types-anxiety-disorders-classified.
2. "Cortisol (Blood)," Health Encyclopedia, University of Rochester Medical Center, www.urmc.rochester.edu

/encyclopedia/content.aspx?contenttypeid=167&contentid
=cortisol_serum.

3. "More Laughter May Be Just What the Doctor Ordered,"
Los Angeles Times, January 31, 1991, www.latimes.com
/archives/la-xpm-1991-01-31-vw-587-story.html.

4. Charmaine Liebertz, "A Healthy Laugh," *Scientific American*,
October 1, 2005, www.scientificamerican.com/article
/a-healthy-laugh.

5. Liebertz, "Healthy Laugh." And University of Turku, "Social
Laughter Releases Endorphins in the Brain," ScienceDaily,
June 1, 2017, www.sciencedaily.com/releases/2017/06
/170601124121.htm.

6. Proverbs 17:22, NKJV.

7. Nehemiah 8:10.

8. "MTHFR Gene," Genetics Home Reference, US National
Library of Medicine, January 21, 2020, https://ghr.nlm.nih
.gov/gene/MTHFR.

9. Traci Stein, PhD, "A Genetic Mutation That Can Affect
Mental and Physical Health," *Psychology Today*, September 5,
2014, www.psychologytoday.com/us/blog/the-integrationist
/201409/genetic-mutation-can-affect-mental-physical-health.

10. Stein, "Genetic Mutation."

11. Stein, "Genetic Mutation."

12. Robert Murray McCheyne, *The Sermons of the Rev. Robert
Murray McCheyne* (New York: Robert Carter & Brothers,
1854), 79.

13. "Exercise for Stress and Anxiety," Anxiety and Depression
Association of America, https://adaa.org/living-with
-anxiety/managing-anxiety/exercise-stress-and-anxiety.

14. Psalm 37:23, NKJV.

10: Walking in Circles

1. Mark Twain, *Roughing It* (Berkeley: University of California Press, 1993), 207–8.
2. Natalie Wolchover, "Why Do Humans Walk in Circles?," Live Science, August 5, 2011, www.livescience.com/33431 -why-humans-walk-circles.html.
3. Wolchover, "Why Do Humans Walk in Circles?"
4. Psalm 119:105, NKJV.
5. Genesis 3:4–5.
6. Romans 8:1.
7. Philippians 4:6–7, NLT.
8. Philippians 4:8, NLT.
9. 1 Corinthians 2:11–12.
10. 2 Corinthians 10:3–5, NKJV.
11. 2 Timothy 1:7, NKJV.

11: Lost and Found

1. Robert Earle Howells, "Lost on the Hiking Trail? 6 Ways to Improve Your Chances of Getting Found," *Los Angeles Times*, August 2, 2019, www.latimes.com/lifestyle /story/2019-08-02/hikers-that-get-lost.
2. Luke 19:10.
3. See Luke 15.

ABOUT THE AUTHOR

. . . .

BECKY THOMPSON is the national bestselling author of the books *Hope Unfolding, Love Unending, Truth Unchanging, My Real Story,* and *Midnight Mom Devotional.* She is the founder of the Midnight Mom Devotional online community, where more than one million moms come together in nightly prayer. Becky also shares hope-filled truth through her top Christian podcast, *Revived Motherhood.* She has a bachelor of science degree in biblical studies and has spent years studying communication, and her heart is to help women encounter Jesus. Originally from Oklahoma, Becky and her family spent two years living in Los Angeles, and now live just outside of Nashville, Tennessee. Becky and her husband, Jared, have three children, Kolton, Kadence, and Jaxton.

ABOUT THE TYPE

· ·

This book was set in Jenson, one of the earliest print type-faces. After hearing of the invention of printing in 1458, Charles VII of France sent coin engraver Nicolas Jenson (c. 1420–80) to study this new art. Not long afterward, Jenson started a new career in Venice in letter-founding and print-ing. In 1471, Jenson was the first to present the form and proportion of this roman font that bears his name.

More than five centuries later, Robert Slimbach, develop-ing fonts for the Adobe Originals program, created Adobe Jenson based on Nicolas Jenson's Venetian Renaissance type-face. It is a dignified font with graceful and balanced strokes.

Encouragement for a Momma's Heart

JOIN THE NIGHTLY
GLOBAL PRAYER MOVEMENT
with *Mommas Just Like You*

*The end of the day can bring so many
feelings to the surface of a momma's heart.
Pray alongside a community of women
who feel just like you do.*

WATERBROOK | MidnightMomDevotional.com